FOCUS ON SUCCESS

Ausgabe Wirtschaft

Workbook

5th edition

von
Michael Benford
Michael Macfarlane
Nicole Hyde
Isobel Williams

unter Mitarbeit der Verlagsredaktion

 Dieses Symbol verweist auf Audios zum Download:
Einfach auf www.cornelsen.de/webcodes gehen,
den Webcode **FOSW-WB-AUDIO** aufrufen
und auf den Link zu den Audiodateien klicken.

FOCUS ON SUCCESS
Ausgabe Wirtschaft

Verfasser/innen:	Michael Benford, Bochum
	Michael Macfarlane, Oxford
	Nicole Hyde, Berlin
	Isobel Williams, Berlin
Projektleitung:	Andreas Goebel
Verlagsredaktion:	Kari-ann Warnakulasuriya
Außenredaktion:	Katinka Welz, Ingolstadt
Redaktionelle Mitarbeit:	Thomas Adam, Elise Nelson
Umschlaggestaltung:	Klein & Halm Grafikdesign, Berlin
Layout:	Oxana Rödel, Absatz DTP-Service, Teltow
Technische Umsetzung:	vitaledesign, Berlin
Coverfoto:	Shutterstock / asiastock
Illustrationen:	Oxford Designers & Illustrators

Erhältlich sind auch:

Schülerbuch	ISBN 978-3-06-451668-7
Handreichungen zum Unterricht mit Unterrichtsmanager (UM) und MP3-CD	ISBN 978-3-06-451670-0
Vocabulary practice book	ISBN 978-3-06-451079-1
Vokabeltrainer-App	für Android, Apple und Windows im jeweiligen App-Store

Soweit in diesem Lehrwerk Personen fotografisch abgebildet sind und ihnen von der Redaktion fiktive Namen, Berufe, Dialoge und Ähnliches zugeordnet oder diese Personen in bestimmte Kontexte gesetzt werden, dienen diese Zuordnungen und Darstellungen ausschließlich der Veranschaulichung und dem besseren Verständnis des Inhalts.

www.cornelsen.de

Die dem Lernmittel beigefügte CD enthält ausschließlich optionale Unterrichtsmaterialien.
Die CD unterliegt nicht dem staatlichen Zulassungsverfahren.

1. Auflage, 1. Druck 2017

Alle Drucke dieser Auflage sind inhaltlich unverändert und können im Unterricht nebeneinander verwendet werden.

© 2017 Cornelsen Verlag GmbH, Berlin

Druck: AZ Druck und Datentechnik GmbH, Kempten

ISBN 978-3-06-451669-4

PEFC zertifiziert
Dieses Produkt stammt aus nachhaltig
bewirtschafteten Wäldern und kontrollierten
Quellen.
www.pefc.de
PEFC/04-31-2260

CONTENTS

1 TALKING ABOUT CELEBRITY

Underline twelve English words you can use when you talk about celebrities. The words are all on pages 6 and 7 of the student's book.

UPFF<u>ANS</u>MXOPAPARAZZIGRLFAMOUSTSTATUSYSTARPLUXURYMLLEGENDZUSTALKERPKACTORMIMAGELBKMAUTOGRAPHCPOPULARITY

2 GETTING IT RIGHT
→ Position of adverbs of time, SB S. 273

Choose the correct position (**A** or **B**) for the adverb of time in the brackets.

1 John **A** spends too much money **B** on fan articles. (always)
2 The paparazzi **A** wait for celebrities **B** outside clubs and bars. (usually)
3 **A** I **B** read about celebrities' problems in the newspapers. (regularly)
4 My favourite singer **A** performs **B** in my town. (never)
5 The group is **A** on the radio **B** (every day)
6 Celebrities **A** love to see their names in the news **B**. (usually)
7 Paparazzi **A** get very rich **B** with their photos. (sometimes)
8 Some stars **A** are **B** on tour. (always)

3 GETTING IT RIGHT
→ Simple present, SB S. 249

Complete the story using the verbs in brackets in the simple present. Take care with questions and negatives.

Briony and Holly Banks ___*are*___ ¹ (be) twins. They both ___*love*___ ²
(love) to dance and they ___*have*___ ³ (have) a lot of talent. They
___*enter*___ ⁴ (enter) a talent show competition.

On the night of the show, Briony ___*sees*___ ⁵ (see) that her sister

isin't ~~wasn't being~~ ___ ⁶ (not be happy). 'What ___*is*___ ⁷ (be)

the problem, Holly?' she ___*asked*___ ⁸ (ask). 'I ___*am scared*___ ⁹
(be scared),' Holly ___*tells*___ ¹⁰ (tell) her.

When the girls ___*come*___ ¹¹ (come) on stage, one of the judges
___*smiles*___ ¹² (smile) kindly. 'Just ___*relax*___ ¹³ (relax),' he ___*says*___ ¹⁴ (say). Holly suddenly ___*feels*___ ¹⁵

(feel) great and she and her sister ___*win*___ ¹⁶ (win) the competition.

4 ASKING QUESTIONS
→ Simple present, SB S. 249; Question words, SB S. 222

Read the answers a celebrity fashion model gave during a TV interview in London. Use the correct forms of *be* and *do* together with the question words from the box to complete the interviewer's questions. Use each question word only once.

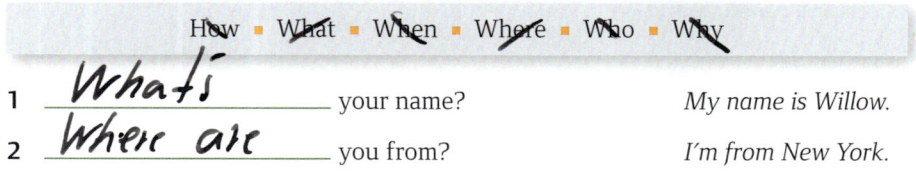

How ▪ What ▪ When ▪ Where ▪ Who ▪ Why

1 ___*What's*___ your name? *My name is Willow.*
2 ___*Where are*___ you from? *I'm from New York.*

3	_How do_	you like London?	_I love London._
4	_Why are_	you in London today?	_I'm in London today to model some clothes._
5	_When do_	you usually start work?	_I usually start work at 6 am._
6	_Who is_	your favourite designer?	_My favourite designer is Marco._

5 BUILDING SKILLS

→ Vorbereitung auf das Lesen, SB S. 214

Before you read the text below, study the clues on the page and then choose the best ending to complete the following statement.

The article is about a celebrity who
  a   believes the media are always nice to her because she is famous.
  b   knows from experience that being a celebrity is not always fun.
  c   pays reporters and paparazzi to give her the attention she wants.

SKILLS CHECKLIST: Predicting

- ☑ Have I read the title?
- ☑ Have I looked at the photo?
- ☑ Have I read the caption under the photo?

FAME – IS IT WORTH IT?

A lot of stories about Desirée, last month's winner of _Stars for Tomorrow_, are appearing in the tabloid newspapers at the moment. Talking openly to _Fame and Fortune_ magazine, the slim, sexy singer explains why media attention is not always a good thing.

5 'Everybody is talking about my relationship with Patrick Strong, one of the judges on the show,' she says. 'I know that when you're a celebrity, you have to give up a lot of your private life. The fans want to know what you're doing,' she says. 'Sometimes things appear in the papers that you don't like, but you learn to accept it. Say you're having a bad day, and
10 someone takes your picture and sells it to the media, that's part of the life of a celebrity,' she continues.

'Some of the stories appearing in the press at the moment are just too personal, though. Now that Patrick and I are close, I'm scared to leave the house because I know the reporters and the paparazzi are
15 waiting for me. They are making my life hard at the moment.'

(182 words)

'You know that the media is interested in your private life when you're a celebrity, but I did not expect it to be this bad.'

6 LOOKING AT THE TEXT

→ Rezeption: Leseverstehen, SB S. 214

Say if these statements are true (T) or false (F). Correct the wrong statements.

1	Desirée is currently appearing in _Stars for Tomorrow_.	F	She appeared on the show last Month Currently in the NewsPaper
2	Desirée knows Patrick well because he is her cousin.	F	She is currently dating him
3	Desirée understands that her fans are interested in her.	✓	

4 She does not want paparazzi to take photos when she is looking bad.

☐ _____

_____

_____

5 The media is full of reports about Desirée's professional plans at the moment.

☐ _____

_____

_____

6 Desirée is unhappy about the attention the press is giving her at the moment.

☐ _____

_____

_____

7 GETTING IT RIGHT → Present progressive, SB S. 249

A Complete the transcript of a phone call between Desirée and Patrick with the words and phrases in brackets. Put the verbs in the present progressive.

Desirée Hi Patrick.

Patrick Hi Desirée. I _am calling_ ¹ (call) from my car. What _are you doing_ (you do) at the moment?

Desirée I _am reading_ ³ (read) the latest report about us in the newspaper.

Patrick What story _does the press m.u.n_ ⁴ (the press make up) now? _is the press..._

Desirée That you _dated_ ⁵ (date) another woman. _are dating_

Patrick These people _go to far!_ ⁶ (go too far). _They are trying_ ⁷ (they try) to split us up?

Desirée I suppose they _are only doing_ ⁸ (only do) their job. Oh, no! Two reporters _are walking up_ ⁹ (walk up) the path to the front door.

Patrick Don't worry, darling. I _am driving into_ ¹⁰ (drive into) your street right now. I can see them.

B Listen and check.

2

8 GETTING IT RIGHT → Simple present ▪ Present progressive, SB S. 249

Choose the simple present or the present progressive to complete the extract from Desirée's fan blog.

I *work / am working* ¹ on a new album and everything *goes / is going* ² well at the moment. OK, I *have / am having* ³ some trouble with the press. The paparazzi *stalk / are stalking* ⁴ me from morning till night and some reporters *look / are looking* ⁵ in the window right now. So what? I *know / am knowing* ⁶ that none of you *believe / are believing* ⁷ the stories in the papers. I *love / am loving* ⁸ you all.

Desirée ♥

1 TALKING ABOUT SPORT

A Unscramble the letters to make words and expressions to talk about sport. Some letters have already been given. All the words and expressions are on page 12 of the student's book.

1 cipainpratt   P _ R _ _ C _ _ _ _ T

2 acesportt   _ _ E _ T _ _ R _

3 labofolt   _ O _ _ A _ _

4 alpy nestin   _ A _ _ _ N _ _

5 proustp a meat   _ _ _ P _ _ _ _ A _ _ E _ _

6 peek-ift avicetisit   _ _ E _ - _ _ _ _ A _ _ _ _ _ _ T _ S

7 od cabeiors   _ O _ _ R _ _ C _ _

8 og gigjong   _ _ _ _ O _ _ _ G

B Complete the dialogue with six of the words/expressions.

A Hello, Ben. I haven't seen you for ages. How are you? You look very well. Do you still do your

_____¹?

B Yes. I _____² at the gym twice a week and I _____³

in the park every morning. I took part in a charity run last Saturday. That's the first time I've been a

_____⁴ in an event like that. It was a lot of fun. But what about you? You used

to be very keen on _____⁵. Do you still play for a team?

A No. I sometimes kick a ball around with my mates, but I stopped playing seriously ages ago. I still

go to matches, but I'm only a _____⁶ these days. I prefer to watch other people

doing the hard work.

2 GETTING IT RIGHT
→ Simple past, SB S. 251

Complete the sentences with the simple past form of the underlined verb. Be careful with irregular forms.

1 I normally <u>go</u> to the gym twice a week. Last week, I only _____ once.

2 We usually <u>play</u> tennis outside. Yesterday, we _____ in the hall.

3 The team doesn't often <u>win</u> their matches, but they _____ last Saturday.

4 The match usually <u>begins</u> at 3 pm, but last week it _____ at 3.30 pm.

5 Where did you <u>buy</u> your running shoes? I _____ them at RunFast.

6 Did you <u>take part</u> in the event this year? Yes. I _____ as usual.

3 GETTING IT RIGHT
→ Present perfect, SB S. 253

A Use the correct form of the verb in brackets to complete the sentences. Circle the signal words.

1 Claire _has left_¹ (leave) our swimming club. She _____² (just move) to

another town.

2 Paul _____¹ (not arrive) yet. He _____²

(never be) late for a game before.

3 _____¹ (you / hear) the news already? Mark Miller _____

_____² (just join) our local ice hockey team.

4 _____¹ (you / meet) our new player, Jan, yet? She _____²

(play) squash in competitions all over the country.

B Complete the expressions with *for* or *since*.   → *For, since*, SB S. 254

1 _____ six years   5 _____ last week

2 _____ a long time   6 _____ we moved to Berlin

3 _____ Easter   7 _____ 21 June

4 _____ a couple of hours 8 _____ ever

4 GETTING IT RIGHT   → Simple past ▪ Present perfect, SB S. 254

Cross out the incorrect version of the verb to complete the text. Circle the expressions that helped you decide. The first one has been done for you.

(Earlier today), the Anti-Doping Agency charged / ~~has charged~~¹ another sports personality with using performance-enhancing drugs. Up till now, the agency did not say / has not said² who the celebrity sportsperson is. According to an insider, however, people from the agency searched / have searched³ the home of one of the country's top runners earlier this week.

The runner, who won / has won⁴ a lot of prizes during his career, told / has told⁵ us in a telephone interview yesterday, that he and another runner only drank / have drunk⁶ a fruit juice before the event. The fruit-juice company sponsored / has sponsored⁷ both runners for over two years. This morning, in a press conference, a spokesperson for the company said / has said⁸: 'Doping in sport was / has been⁹ a problem for years but the drinks we gave / have given¹⁰ the runners before the race were / have been¹¹ pure fruit juice, as always. None of our drinks ever contained / have ever contained¹² drugs.'

5 GETTING IT RIGHT   → Pronouns, SB S. 268

A Complete each message using a subject or an object pronoun for the underlined words.

EXAMPLE: There is a message from your parents on the answering machine.
Can you listen to ___*it*___ and call ___*them*___ back?

1 Joe is working late and can't come to football practice.

Can you call _____ at the office?

2 I am playing in a hockey team at the moment.

Would you like you to watch _____ play?

3 Clara knows you have some new tennis balls.

_____¹ would like to borrow _____².

4 We have a problem with the CD player.

Can you help _____¹ fix _____²?

5 Some people say that Zumba is fun. Jessica and I are going to try Zumba.

_____¹ say that Zumba is fun. _____² are going to try _____³.

B Read Ann's blog post about her dance class and find the pronouns. Highlight the subject pronouns in yellow, the object pronouns in green and the possessive adjectives in blue. The first three have been done for you. Now you only have to find 22 more.

Here's some news about <mark>my</mark> dance class. <mark>We</mark> have a new instructor. <mark>Her</mark> name is Alice. She's a really good teacher. Dancing is a great way to keep fit and have fun. It's also a great way to meet people. There are ten of us in the class. A few weeks ago, a boy called Tim had a
5　problem with one of his shoes. Its *sole* [Sohle] broke and this made him fall and crash into me. Those of you who follow this blog know that I've always liked him, but this was the first time he noticed me. It wasn't long till we started going out. His parents have invited us to visit them next weekend in their new home. They have just moved to Glasgow.
10　If you want to join the dance class, send me your email address.

6　BUILDING SKILLS

→ Rezeption: Hörverstehen, SB S. 225

A **You are going to listen to three people talk about how they keep fit. Before you listen, look at the photos and study the questions on the notepad below. Then choose the expressions from this list that you think you will hear.**

1　strengthens the heart and the lungs
2　no fun at all
3　reduce stress
4　a fun way to keep fit
5　exercise every bit of your body
6　get slim and stay slim
7　it's really boring
8　helps you relax
9　gives you a good feeling

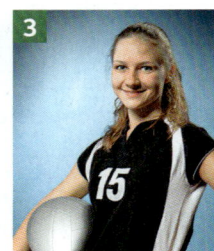

Jane, 26, teacher　　*Will, 22, trainee*　　*Lily, 18, student*

Who	What?	Where?	Health benefits?	Other?
Jane, 26, teacher	_____ _____ ¹	in class; at _____ ²	good for _____, _____ ³, muscles; gets rid of _____ ⁴	fun; not _____ ⁵
Will, 22, trainee	_____ _____ ¹	_____ _____ ²	great _____ ³; relaxing / you _____ ⁴; losing _____ ⁵	swimming helps you get _____ ⁶
Lily, 18, student	_____ _____ ¹	_____ _____ ²	even if you _____ ³ you feel great; _____ ⁴ the calories; working with _____ ⁵ = good feeling	team sport good way to _____ ⁶; made _____ ⁷

B **Now listen and check.**
3

C **Before you listen again, use information from the page to fill in the notepad with as much information as you can. Then listen again and complete the notes.**
3

1 TALKING ABOUT BRANDS

A Translate the words into English to complete the crossword with words you can use to talk about brands. All the words are on pages 18 and 19 of the student's book.

ACROSS:
1 Werbespruch
2 modisch
4 Ware
5 erschwinglich
6 Qualität
9 Wahl

DOWN:
3 Preis
7 Werbung
8 Werte
10 berühmt

B Unscramble the highlighted letters in the crossword to make a two-word expression which says what shoppers often look for.

□□□□□   □□□□□

2 GETTING IT RIGHT

→ Adjectives ▪ Adverbs of manner, SB S. 270

A Adjective or adverb? Underline the correct form.

1 If you don't have much money, you have to shop careful / carefully.
2 Don't simple / simply buy something because it's been advertised by a star.
3 The clothes look beautiful / beautifully when they're on a model.
4 It is usual / usually safer to buy a brand-name computer.
5 These jeans look similar / similarly to the ones I saw advertised last week.
6 Expensive / expensively products don't always last longer than goods you buy cheap / cheaply.

B Underline the adverbs below then unscramble the words to make sentences. Make sure you put the adverbs in the correct positions.

1 at the outlet store / frequently / Lucy / shops

_____

2 always / dresses / Jim / well

_____

3 my new computer / stopped / suddenly / working

_____

4 good / in that café / is / the coffee / usually

_____

5 I / these boots / really / want

_____

3 USING A DICTIONARY → Ein Wörterbuch benutzen, SB S. 217; Vokabeln lernen, SB S. 220

Complete the table using your dictionary. The words are from page 19 of the student's book.

Noun	Verb	Adjective
choice	_____ 1	_____ 2
cost	_____ 3	_____ 4
_____ 5	_____ 6	affordable

4 GETTING IT RIGHT → Comparison of adjectives and adverbs, SB S. 271

A Joe is shopping for a new smartphone. Use information from the table to complete his thoughts with the correct form of the words in brackets. Add *as ... as* or *... than* where necessary.

	Universe	NeatPhone	Bright
dimensions	142mm × 73mm × 8.1mm	124mm × 59mm × 7.6mm	160mm × 84mm × 8.4mm
weight	145gr	112gr	206gr
battery life	+++++	+++	++++
price	€650	€600	€585

Oh, dear. I'm not sure which of these three phones to choose. I can see that the Universe is _bigger than_ 1 (big) the NeatPhone and the Bright is the _biggest_ 2 (big) of all three, but I'll have to think some more. How heavy are they? The NeatPhone is _____ 3 (light) the two other phones. The Universe is not _____ 4 (heavy) the Bright. The Bright is _____ 5 (heavy) the other two.

What does it say here about the battery life? The battery life of the NeatPhone is not _____ 6 (long) the battery life of the Bright. It looks as if the batteries of the Universe last _____ 7 (long).

What about the price? Well, the Bright is the _____ 8 (cheap) of the phones. The NeatPhone is _____ 9 (expensive) the Bright, and the Universe is the _____ 10 (expensive) of them all. Oh, I don't know which of these three phones is _____ 11 (good). Choosing a phone is one of the _____ 12 (difficult) things to do in life. Hmmm. I think I'll buy the ...

B Now listen and check.

C Listen again. Which phone does Joe choose and why?

11

5 COLLOCATIONS

→ Ein Wörterbuch benutzen, SB S. 217

Cross out the word which you cannot use to form a collocation with the word in capital letters.

1 current ▪ high ▪ latest ▪ low ▪ newest FASHION
2 famous ▪ leading ▪ popular ▪ victim ▪ well-known BRAND
3 best ▪ good ▪ poor ▪ new ▪ top QUALITY
4 blue ▪ copies ▪ designer ▪ skinny ▪ tight JEANS
5 DESIGNER clothes ▪ house ▪ jeans ▪ label ▪ name

6 BUILDING SKILLS

→ Interaktion: An Diskussionen teilnehmen, SB S. 246

A How good is your knowledge of phrases for discussion? Without checking the back flap of the student's book, write at least one phrase for each heading.

SKILLS CHECKLIST: Phrases for discussions

☑ Have I learned suitable phrases for discussion?
☑ Do I know how and when to use them?

| Giving an opinion | Giving reasons | Agreeing with an opinion |

| Disagreeing with an opinion | Interrupting |

B Circle the correct word in brackets to complete the sentences.

1 My own (reason / view) of the matter is that it's fun to wear the latest fashions.
2 In my (meaning / opinion), the style doesn't suit everyone.
3 The main (reason / idea) is that the clothes are too expensive for teenagers.
4 I'm sorry, but I have to (agree / disagree) with you on that point. Expensive T-shirts don't always last longer than cheap ones.
5 I'm (afraid / concerned) I can't accept that. A designer watch will last forever.
6 Can I just (interrupt / tell) you for a moment? I strongly (agree / believe) that you have to spend money to look good.

C Imagine that you are going to take part in a discussion about whether to buy designer or regular jeans and why. Complete the cards with arguments for and against designer jeans and regular jeans.

Designer jeans		Regular jeans	
for	**against**	**for**	**against**
fit better, …	*expensive, …*	*inexpensive, …*	*poor quality, …*

D Now decide on your point of view and make some notes that you could use in a discussion on the question.

Jeans are jeans. The only difference is the name.

Designer jeans last longer and fit better.

SKILLS CHECKLIST: Group discussions

☑ Have I thought about what I want to say?
☑ Have I prepared some bullet points?
☑ Have I written down key phrases in English?

E If you have the chance, carry out the discussion with two or three other people. Check with your teacher if you can do this in class.

4 Leisure and free time

1 TALKING ABOUT FREE TIME ACTIVITIES

Complete the mindmap with free time activities.

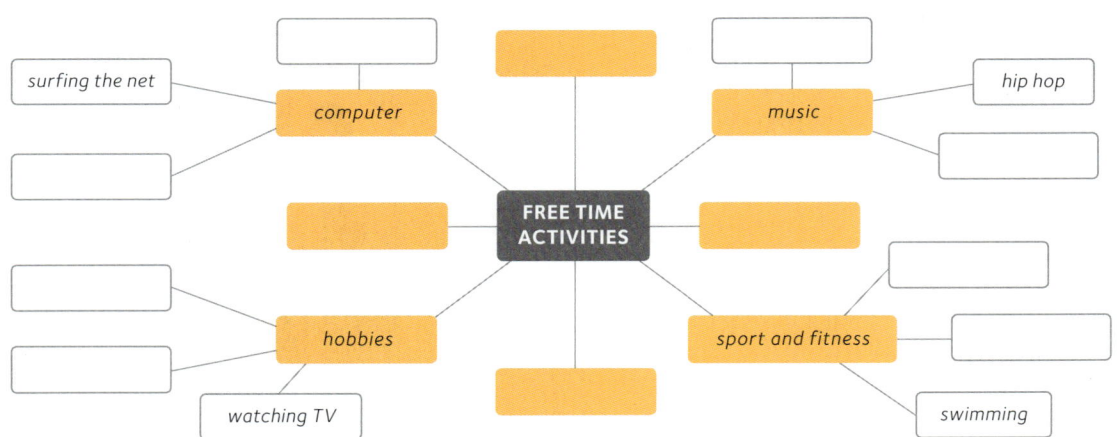

2 GETTING IT RIGHT

→ *Will* future ▪ *Going to* future, SB S. 257

A Fill in the correct form of the *will* future.

1 **A** _____ ¹ (you come) with me to the pop festival tomorrow?

B Probably not. The weather reporter said there _____ ² (probably be) a storm in the evening.

A Oh, no! I hope it _____ ³ (not be) stormy. If it is, the organizers

_____ ⁴ (cancel) the festival.

2 **A** It's disco night at the youth club. _____ ⁵ (I see) you there later?

B No, I _____ ⁶ (not have) time this evening. I have to do my homework.

A Come on! I _____ ⁷ (help) you. Then we _____ ⁸ (be able to) go together.

B Use the notes to make sentences using the *going to* future.

EXAMPLE: Jane / join / salsa class / this winter   _Jane is going to join a salsa class this winter._

1   I / train for / next marathon

_____

2   Mark and Mindy / go backpacking / Australia / next summer

_____

3   some pupils / start / film club / next term

_____

4   snooker championships / be held / Paris / this year

_____

5   you / really / buy / motorbike?

_____

6   I / not go shopping / for the rest of the year

_____

3 **BUILDING SKILLS** → Produktion: Cartoons beschreiben und analysieren, SB S. 236

A **Choose the correct words from the brackets to complete the description of the cartoon.**

The cartoon shows a teenage boy and his mother in a living room. The boy _____¹ (is lying / lies) on the sofa. He _____² (has / is) overweight. He _____ _____³ (is looking / looks) frightened because a group of vultures [Geier] _____⁴ (are watching / watch) him _____⁵ (hungry / hungrily). Through the open window, we can see that two more vultures _____⁶ (fly / are flying) to join their friends. The boy's mother _____⁷ (stands / is standing) behind her son. She appears to be _____⁸ (angry / angrily). She _____⁹ (shouts / is shouting) the words that are written under the cartoon.

"Maybe if you showed some sign of life once in a while this sort of thing wouldn't happen."

B **Complete the interpretation of the cartoon with one of the sentence endings below.**

The joke is that …
a mothers don't understand anything about relaxing.
b some kids are so lazy that they appear to be dead.
c some vultures have come to eat an overweight boy.

SKILLS CHECKLIST: Interpreting a cartoon

☑ Have I read the caption?
☑ Have I described everything in the cartoon?
☑ Have I used the present progressive to describe what is happening?

4 **LOOKING AT THE TEXT** → Rezeption: Leseverstehen, SB S. 214

Jenny, 16, often uses her blog to talk about her problems with her parents.

Read the post and say if the following statements are true (T) or false (F).

1 Jenny enjoys listening to how her parents behaved when they were teenagers. ☐

2 She doesn't use any social networks. ☐

3 She likes to meet her friends outside after school. ☐

4 According to Jenny, you can find out about a lot of things on the Internet. ☐

5 She doesn't want to have contact with people online. ☐

6 She would like the older generation to be more tolerant towards teenagers. ☐

'When I was your age …'

How often have you heard this in the last few weeks? You're chilling, lying on the sofa, listening to music or checking some post and – bang! – all the good feelings disappear and you have to listen to how life was in the old days. Everybody wrote letters and if you wanted to chat, you sat on the step and spoke to the kids next door. So what? History is interesting, but things change and develop. →

5 Kids today use social networking. I don't have to be with my friends in person to have a conversation, I can video call them. I don't need go to my mate's house and tell him about a great new band, I can post a link to it in our Facebook group.

It's not all about having fun. We also use social networking to discuss schoolwork and to exchange ideas. We are open to other people's ideas and enjoy mixing with people from different groups.

10 I wish people would just understand that things are different today. I mean, when my parents and grandparents were growing up they didn't even have computers!

Perhaps, when older people start a sentence with, 'When I was your age …' they should try to end it with the words, 'I was a teenager, too.'

(214 words)

5 BUILDING SKILLS

→ Schriftliche Mediation, SB S. 240

Ein Freund hat Ihnen erzählt, dass seine Mutter ständig zu ihm sagt: „Als ich in deinem Alter war…!". Schreiben Sie eine E-Mail an diesen Freund und erzählen Sie ihm von Jennys Blog aus Übung 4, und erläutern Sie Jennys Anregungen zu diesem Thema.

SKILLS CHECKLIST: Written mediation

☑ Have I read the situation?
☑ Have I understood who the mediation is for?
☑ Have I written the right sort of text?

6 GETTING IT RIGHT

→ Quantifiers, SB S. 274

Choose the correct words from the brackets to complete the dialogues.

1 **A** Did you see _____¹ (any / some) interesting programmes on TV last night?

   B I don't watch _____² (many / much) TV. I do so many other things and there's too

   _____³ (few / little) time to fit everything in.

2 **A** I go to the gym _____⁴ (a few / a little) times a week. What about you?

   B I go to the gym, too. There are often _____⁵ (any / some) interesting people there.

3 **A** Does your college offer _____⁶ (many / much) after-school activities?

   B No, they don't offer _____⁷ (any / some). Not _____⁸ (many / much) people

   are interested.

4 **A** We have _____⁹ (a few / a little) time before the dance class starts. Can you show me

   _____¹⁰ (any / some) moves?

   B If you like. How _____¹¹ (many / much) moves do you know already?

   A Not _____¹² (many / much). I've only been here _____¹³ (a few / a little) times and

   I don't practise _____¹⁴ (many / much) at home.

7 BUILDING SKILLS

→ Produktion: Bilder beschreiben und analysieren, SB S. 236

Describe the photo, relating it to the topic of the unit. Explain why you would (not) enjoy the activity shown.

SKILLS CHECKLIST: Describing a picture

☑ Have I described the people in the picture?
☑ Have I described the atmosphere?

1 WORKING WITH WORDS

Fill in the gaps with some of the highlighted words from the text on pages 36 and 37 of the student's book.

_____¹ of how old you are – you can be a child or an _____² – you're never too old to open a social media account. There are _____³ to choose from, e.g. Facebook, Twitter, LinkedIn or Instagram. At first sight they _____⁴ to be very different, but they are the same in many ways. This is because they let people _____⁵ with each other and help them feel less cut off and _____⁶.

A recent _____⁷ conducted by an online bank has shown that on _____⁸, Britons spend at least one hour on the Internet per day. In some cases, the amount of time spent on social media _____⁹ two hours. For these reasons, many people open a social media account to _____¹⁰ being forgotten by their friends.

2 LOOKING AT THE TEXT

→ Rezeption: Leseverstehen, SB S. 214

Answer these questions on the text on pages 36 and 37 of the student's book in your own words.

1 How much time does the average British adult or child spend on social media every day?

_____

2 How are the social media habits of men and women different?

_____

3 How many Britons use Twitter for more than two hours a day?

_____

4 Which social media platform is most popular? How do we know?

_____

5 How do some people make sure they are not cut off from their friends?

_____

6 What is Rebecca Dye's job?

_____

7 What does Rebecca Dye probably mean when she says 'at the expense of other communications'?

_____

8 How will Rebecca Dye's company interact more with its customers in future?

_____

3 BUILDING SKILLS

→ Rezeption: Leseverstehen – Grobverständnis, SB S. 214

A **Study the box on the right, then skim the text and decide which of the following statements best summarizes it.**

a Social media only played a small part in the volunteers' lives.

b Only the lonely use Facebook and Twitter.

c Giving up social media can make room for other things.

d Social media use is a bad habit that must be broken.

SKILLS CHECKLIST: Skimming

- ☑ Have I read the title carefully?
- ☑ Have I read all of the first paragraph?
- ☑ Have I read the first sentence of all the other paragraphs?
- ☑ Have I read all of the final paragraph?

FACEBOOK AND TWITTER ADDICTS GO 'COLD TURKEY' IN MAJOR EXPERIMENT

The research project focused on a month-long experiment where 40 people from across the UK were forced to change their normal social media behaviours. A number of Facebook and Twitter *addicts* suffered a range of *withdrawal symptoms* after being forced to deactivate their accounts for a month.

5   Many described extreme feelings of isolation because of the reduced contact with friends or family, while others said they were frustrated at losing their key communication tool. Some users lost contact with friends and family because they had no contact details other than a Facebook address.

    As one female *volunteer* from Yorkshire *admitted*: 'So much of my life was organised via
10 Facebook. I haven't communicated with my family all week.' Another of the volunteers said: 'I've felt alone and cut off from the world. My fingers seem to be programmed to seek out the Facebook app every time I pick up my phone.'

    Social media addicts had to find other ways to spend their time. A woman from Wales said being taken off Facebook had allowed her to focus on the household, while another volunteer
15 *confessed* the 'ban' had allowed her to spend more time with her daughter.   (195 words)

Vocabulary notes

cold turkey	*kalter Entzug*	withdrawal symptoms	*Entzugserscheinungen*	to admit	*zugeben*
addict	*Süchtige(r)*	volunteer	*Freiwillige(r)*	to confess	*gestehen*

B Read the text again and make a list of the following:

1 the withdrawal symptoms people felt   **2** the things that some people started to do again

4 GETTING IT RIGHT   → Simple past, SB S. 251

Put the underlined verbs into the simple past. Use the list of irregular verbs on page 349 of the student's book to help you.

SARAH GETS A SHOCK

Sarah goes _____[1] online, opens _____[2] her Facebook account and checks _____[3] her messages. She finds _____[4] one with a picture of herself at a party and is _____[5] shocked. At first, she thinks _____[6] there is _____[7] only one message, but then she finds _____[8] another and another. She doesn't _____[9] know what to do.

    At school, she sits _____[10] in the classroom and looks _____[11] around her. Are _____[12] these people her friends or her enemies now? How much do _____[13] they know about her? Sarah doesn't _____[14] notice the teacher and can't _____[15] answer his questions. The bell rings _____[16] and the lesson is _____[17] over. Sarah leaves _____[18] the classroom and understands _____[19] one thing: She must _____[20] tell someone, but who?

5 LISTENING

→ Rezeption: Hörverstehen, SB S. 225

A **Listen to the phone call between Mrs Seale and the mother who brought her son to the party and say if the following statements are true or false. Correct the false statements.**

1 Catherine Seale phones Margaret Green.
2 The two women's sons are in the same class at school.
3 Margaret Green knows that the Seales are on holiday in France.
4 Margaret Green is in the front garden of Catherine's house.
5 Christopher told his mother he planned to throw a party.
6 The party is out of control.
7 The riot police are trying to break into the house through the roof.
8 The riot police are blocking the street.
9 Catherine's son planned to pay a bouncer to make sure only the right guests got in.
10 Mrs Green stopped the people wrecking the front garden.

B **Listen again and complete the sentences with the words you hear. They are also in the text on page 40 of the student's book.**

Margaret   There are young people everywhere, some are drunk and _____¹ in the

front garden.

Margaret   I think the boy on the roof is trying to open the _____².

Catherine   On my new carpet! They'll _____³ it!

Margaret   I would say hundreds. I'm so sorry to tell you all this but I think they must be

_____⁴.

Margaret   I can't see him. He must be inside but I don't want to go in there with all those drunken

_____⁵.

Catherine   My husband has been listening and we're getting the first _____⁶

back to London!

C **Expand the notes below into Mrs Green's account of what she saw at the Seales' house.**

○ ○

Margaret Green drove – Jamie – party – Christopher Seale's house
When – (arrive) she (see) hundreds of young people – street – front garden
The music – (be) extremely loud
Jamie – (get) out – car – (walk) – house – (ring) – doorbell – (wait)
Nobody – (open) – door – (push) – open – (go) inside
When – door (open) – Mrs Green (see) – dancing – shouting
Suddenly – (hear) – crash
It – (come) – roof
She – (look) up – (see) – teenager – roof
The next thing – (see) – riot police
They – (jump) out of – vans – (start) – break up – outside the house
Mrs Green – (realise) – things – (be) out of control – (phoned) – Catherine Seale
She – (think) – the Seales – (be) out for the evening
She – (not know) – they (be) – holiday – France

6 **GETTING IT RIGHT**

→ Simple past ▪ Present perfect, SB S. 254

Complete the sentences with the simple past or the present perfect.

1 Sarah (not use) _____ Facebook for over twelve months now.

2 She last (use) _____ it last year.

3 Since then she (change) _____ ¹ schools and (make) _____ ²
   new friends.

4 The first few weeks at her new school (not be) _____ ¹ easy but after a month or

   so she (feel) _____ ² at home.

5 When she (tell) _____ ¹ her new friends about the cyberbullying, they (be)

   _____ ² shocked.

6 In the past, Sarah (spend) _____ at least three hours a day online.

7 This year she (not be) _____ online at all.

8 Her life (change) _____ a lot since she started at her new school.

9 So far this year she (start) _____ ¹ to play the piano and (do) _____ ²
   a lot more sport.

10 Last week her piano teacher (tell) _____ ¹ her she (play) _____ ²
    well for a beginner.

**Look at the text *Shopping from the couch* on page 44 of the student's book and
rewrite the following sentences to make them true.** → Rezeption: Leseverstehen, SB S. 214

BUSINESS OPTIONS

1 Most people find shopping in a store is a relaxing way to spend their free time.

   _____

2 People who shop online know exactly what store they would like to shop in.

   _____

3 Virtual stores are not allowed to collect information about you.

   _____

4 Online shoppers often feel frustrated browsing
   through virtual aisles trying to find what they
   would like to buy.

   _____

   _____

5 Traditional stationary stores have not been
   affected by the success of online stores.

   _____

   _____

1 LOOKING AT THE TEXT

→ Rezeption: Leseverstehen, SB S. 214

A Look at text A on page 46 of the student's book and then match the sentence halves.

1	VW found that traditional advertising methods	a	use the stairs instead of the escalator.
2	In order to advertise their cars	b	clever, environmentally-friendly technology.
3	VW and their ad agency DDB therefore	c	in Stockholm, Sweden.
4	They started the campaign at a subway station	d	they realised they could play music with them.
5	They wanted to encourage people to	e	were becoming less and less effective.
6	VW made it attractive to use the stairs by	f	it went viral.
7	A lot of commuters chose to use the stairs when	g	VW needed to do something very different.
8	When VW released a video of the musical stairs	h	the public to enter a video competition.
9	After releasing two more viral videos, VW invited	i	invented the 'Fun Theory'.
10	The public now associate VW's cars with	j	making them produce notes like a piano.

B Now read texts B and C on pages 46 and 47 of the student's book and say if the statements are true (T) or false (F). Correct the false statements.

1 Very few people recycle things in Sweden. ☐

2 The bottle bank arcade pays people to recycle their glass. ☐

3 The bottle bank arcade communicates with the public. ☐

4 It is just as successful as a conventional bottle bank. ☐

5 VW and DDB want people to throw more rubbish into rubbish bins. ☐

6 VW and DDB's rubbish bin is always over a deep hole. ☐

7 When you throw something in, you hear a loud noise. ☐

8 The new bin has a maximum capacity of 72kg of rubbish per day. ☐

2 BUILDING SKILLS

→ Präsentieren, SB S. 243

Sevda and Frank have prepared a presentation on a fun solution to encourage people to wear safety belts in cars. However, their notes have got mixed up.

A Look at the *Useful phrases* on page 48 of the student's book and then put the presentation in the right order.

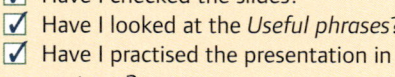

SKILLS CHECKLIST: Presentations

☑ Have I checked the slides?
☑ Have I looked at the *Useful phrases*?
☑ Have I practised the presentation in my team?

☐ a **Frank:** If you have any questions, we'll be pleased to answer them.

☐ b **Sevda:** As you can see from this slide, the dummies are injured because they are not wearing seat belts.

☐ c **Frank:** So how can we encourage people to wear seat belts? In this slide you can see an in-car entertainment screen for back seat passengers, for example children.

☐ d **Sevda:** Good morning. My name's Sevda and this is my colleague Frank.

☐ e **Frank:** Thanks for coming to this presentation.

☐ f **Sevda:** Today we're going to look at the problem of road safety.

☐ g **Frank:** To sum up, this solution makes it fun to be safe.

☐ h **Sevda:** In this slide you can see how a car and the passengers look after a car crash. By the way, this one has dummies, not real passengers.

- [ ] **i** **Sevda:** Let's begin by seeing what happens when a car crashes.
- [ ] **j** **Sevda:** Frank is now going to talk about a fun solution to make people wear seat belts.
- [ ] **k** **Frank:** But it only works if you're wearing your seat belt.
- [ ] **l** **Frank:** Children in the back seat naturally want to use the entertainment system.

B Practise giving the presentation with a partner.

3 LISTENING

→ Rezeption: Hörverstehen, SB S. 225

A Look at your answers to exercise 7A on page 49 of the student's book to make sure you understand what the 4 Ps in the marketing mix are and then write them in column A of the table below.

B Listen to the recording and write down the information you hear to explain what each P refers to in this situation.

A Definition	B Description

4 GETTING IT RIGHT

→ *Will* future ▪ *Going to* future, SB S. 257

A Tom Slater at Ad-Agency Plus in Edinburgh is discussing the launch of a new range of MyStyle wearables. Use the notes to make sentences with the *will* future (predicted actions), the *going to* future (intended actions) or the present progressive (fixed arrangements).

1 I'm sure / wearables / be / great success / near future (prediction)

_____

2 We / launch / the whole range / in Edinburgh / Monday (fixed arrangement)

_____

3 Each member / my team / demonstrate / different sort of wearable (intended action)

_____

4 I / wear / waterproof Android watch (intended action)

_____

5 We / have / press conference / 9 am (fixed arrangement)

_____

6 We / believe / demand for wearables / double / next six months (prediction)

_____

B Tom and his team are presenting MyStyle wearables at a big consumer electronics store in Edinburgh. Complete the sentences using the present progressive (fixed arrangements), the *going to* future (intended actions) or the *will* future (predicted actions).

Good morning and welcome to the launch of MyStyle's range of fantastic new wearables! This morning

_____[1] (introduce) you to a world of clever new products and

we're that sure that _____[2] (make) your life more fun! _____

_____³ (start) by showing you our Bodylife-tracker model. If you wear a Bodylife-tracker,

_____⁴ (be) able to record your physical, social and entertainment activities 24/7.

Top Olympic athlete Jessi Jones wore one for a whole week, and when you watch the video clip, _____

_____⁵ (see) how it works. We all know that Jessi _____⁶

(compete) for the UK in the World Championships next month. _____⁷ (take)

part in six events and we're certain that _____⁸ (win) six medals, so we at

MyStyle wish her good luck! After the video clip, _____⁹ (ask) you to fill in

postcards, so you can all take part in our 'Good Luck Jessi!' draw. We can tell you now that someone here

today _____¹⁰ (win) a free trip for two to the World Championships next month!

5 **BUILDING SKILLS**

→ Scannen nach Einzelinformationen im Text, SB S. 221

A **Study the checklist and then scan the text and answer the questions.**

1 When was Sony founded?
2 How many famous new products did Sony bring out bring out
  between 1955 and 2013?
3 What went wrong in 2011?

SKILLS CHECKLIST: Scanning
☑ Have I read the questions carefully?
☑ Have I focused on one type of information only?

SONY: The history of a household name

5 Ask anyone what they first think of when they hear the word 'Sony' and each generation will tell you something different. _Depending on_ your age, you will say anything _ranging from_ the transistor radio (first made by Sony in 1955) to the Trinitron colour TV (1973), the Walkman (1979), the first CD player (1982), the camcorder (1987), the PlayStation (1994), AIBO the robotic dog (1999) or the first waterproof smartphone, tablet
10 computer and smartwatch (2013).

Sony started to think global as early as 1955 when the Tokyo Tsoshiu Kogyo company changed its brand name to Sony. Suddenly everyone was able to _pronounce_ the Japanese company's name
15 and the Sony logo started to appear all over the world. In 1961 Sony was also the first Japanese company to sell its _shares_ in the US, thereby opening the door to the world's biggest consumer market and preparing the ground for new
20 products.

Since being established by Akio Morita and Masaru Ibuka on 7 May 1946, Sony has consistently changed our lifestyles. Radios used to be large pieces of furniture made of wood which
25 people listened to at home. This changed in 1958 when Sony brought out the legendary portable TR-63 shirt pocket transistor radio described as 'the smallest transistor radio in the world'. People could suddenly listen to the radio anywhere they

30 chose. Up to the end of the 1970s, listening to music had also meant staying in one place because record players, tape recorders and _jukeboxes_ were big and heavy. This changed when Sony's _founder_, Masaru Ibuka asked an audio engineer to make
35 him a portable tape player, so he could listen to opera on _long-haul flights_ from Japan to the US. The first Walkman was born and Sony kept the name for its MiniDisc (1991), MP3 player (2003) and Android Walkman (2012).

40 However, it hasn't always been _plain sailing_. Sony's PlayStation network was hacked in 2011 and personal details from 77 million accounts were _compromised_. The company also stopped selling laptops and PCs in 2014 because they were not
45 making a profit. (343 words)

Vocabulary notes			
depending on	je nach	founder	*Gründer*
ranging from … to	von … über … bis	long-haul flight	*Langstreckenflug*
to pronounce	aussprechen	plain sailing	*einfach, problemlos*
shares	*Aktien*	compromised	*kompromittiert, nicht mehr sicher*
jukebox	*Musikbox*		

B Match the paragraphs with these headings.

> Major setbacks ▪ Famous inventions ▪ World market ▪ Mobile entertainment

C Answer the questions on the text in your own words as far as possible.

1 What two important things happened in 1955?
2 Why was it important for Sony to sell its shares in the US?
3 How did two of Sony's inventions change people's lifestyles?
4 Which market has Sony recently withdrawn from?

6 BUILDING SKILLS → Produktion: Schaubilder beschreiben und analysieren, SB S. 238

Look at the *Building skills* and *Useful phrases* boxes on pages 52 and 53 of the student's book and then complete the sentences about the graph on page 52. Use the simple present, the present perfect or the simple past.

The graph _____¹ (give) us a clear indication of how media ad spending in the US _____

_____² (increase) every year since 2011. It _____³ (rise) fastest in 2012 but then

_____⁴ (go) up more slowly in 2013. In general, the graph _____⁵ (show) us how,

over the years, spending _____⁶ (rise) by hundreds of millions of dollars every year.

The overall trend _____⁷ (be) still upwards, so we can say that American admen still

_____⁸ (not stop) investing large sums of money in media advertising.

Look at the text *Products have lives too!* on page 54 of the student's book and match the definitions (A–E) below with the correct terms (1–5).

BUSINESS OPTIONS

1 Creation and development stage _____

2 Introductory stage _____

3 Growth stage _____

4 Maturity stage _____

5 Decline stage _____

A The product is being sold and the company is earning more and more from its sales.

B The product has done as well as it can at this point and changes are often made so that the product will continue to be popular.

C The product is no longer doing very well and often stops being produced at this point.

D This is the first time the product is presented and no one knows how it will do on the market yet.

E The product is only an idea at this point and needs to be turned into something that can be sold.

1 WORKING WITH WORDS

A Match these words from the text on pages 56 and 57 of the student's book to their opposites (1–8).

> borrow ■ criticize ■ extended ■ forget ■ huge ■ long-distance ■ noisy ■ together

1 lend _____   5 quiet _____

2 local _____   6 remember _____

3 nuclear _____   7 separately _____

4 praise _____   8 tiny _____

B Use pairs of words from part A to complete the following sentences.

1 My grandmother lives nearby in the _____[1] area but my aunt lives in Australia – that means spending a lot of money on _____[2] calls!

2 It's too _____[1] to talk properly here with all the children running around. But it's _____[2] outside, so let's go out there.

3 **A** Did you _____[1] to send Grandad's birthday card on the way home?

   B Oh, no, I'm sorry, I _____[2]. I'll go to the post office now.

4 **A** Are you and your parents going to travel _____[1]?

   B No, we're going _____[2]. They're going by train, and I'm flying.

5 Traditionally, people used to live together as part of a large, _____[1] family, but in the modern world, the small, _____[2] family unit has become much more common.

6 We'd need a _____[1] house if the whole family lived together. There isn't enough room for our grandparents in this _____[2] house!

7 **A** Could I _____[1] some money for a few days?

   B Well, I can _____[2] you €50 until Friday, but I'd have to have it back by then.

8 Why do you always _____[1] the children's school work so much? You need to be more positive and _____[2] them when they get things right.

2 GETTING IT RIGHT

→ Relative clauses, SB S. 269

A Complete the story with the statements in the box. Change them into relative clauses, using *who* or *which*.

> ■ They were offered jobs.   ■ It was very poor.
> ■ It paid very little.   ■ He came to England first.
> ■ He was hiring workers for a UK textile company.   ■ They followed their arrival.
> ■ He never gave up on anything.   ■ It would offer a better future.

Rajeev's Grandad Deepak was the one _____[1].

He and his young wife Mira came from a rural village in northern India _____

_____[2]. They both had jobs at a local textile workshop _____

_____[3]. Not surprisingly, they wanted a new life – a life _____

_____ ⁴. Then one day the village was visited by an agent

_____ ⁵. Deepak and three other men

_____ ⁶ travelled together to Bradford in the

north of England. The months _____ ⁷ were

very difficult, but Deepak was a young man _____ ⁸.

He worked and saved hard and six months later he was able to bring Mira over from India to join him.

B **Now complete the dialogue with the statements in the box. Change them into relative clauses, leaving out _who_ (or _that_) and _which_ (or _that_) where possible.**

■ I've been most worried about them.	■ The company had already got rid of them.
■ I had to go next.	■ It was doing badly.
■ She knew she might soon lose it.	■ It made us decide to move.
■ She pushed for us to move here.	■ The EU financial crisis hit it very badly.

One day, Lisa's dad was talking to Tom, a colleague at work.

Tom So tell me, what brought you over to England?

Dad Well, the thing _____

_____ ¹ was work. You see, my wife

Kim had a job _____

_____ ². As for me, I worked

in Sales for a company _____

_____ ³. There were others

_____ ⁴, and I knew that I might be the one

_____ ⁵.

Tom That must have been a very hard time. Ireland was one of the countries _____

_____ ⁶, wasn't it?

Dad That's right, but I kept hoping our problems would go away. In the end, it was Kim

_____ ⁷.

Tom Are you happy you made the move?

Dad I am now, but it's been hard. It's our children Lisa and Sam _____

_____ ⁸. Especially Lisa. She tries to be cheerful, but I know she's often been

lonely. We're all looking forward to seeing all our family again over Christmas.

3 WRITING AN INFORMAL LETTER

Put the letter parts and sentences in order to write Lisa's letter.

Letter parts
Dublin 22   Lots of Love   29ᵗʰ May, 20..   53 West Road
Lisa   Dear Grandma and Grandpa   Ireland

Sentences
I'll be able to show you them when we get home for Christmas next month.
Well, I must stop now and run to catch the post.
This is to say a big 'thank you' for the money you kindly sent me for my birthday.
I can't wait for that because I miss you and all the family so much.
Thank you again!   So do Mum, Dad and Sam.
I'm going to put it towards some beautiful shoes I really, really want!

4 WORKING WITH WORDS

A Choose the correct preposition of place. There might be more than one correct answer.

1 He was going through the bin _____ (in / at) my bedroom.

2 I had a part-time job _____ (at / in) the little supermarket along the road.

3 I wanted to meet my friends _____ (in / at) town.

4 My grades were dropping because of stress _____ (in / at) home.

B Look at the map and complete the description with these prepositions of place.

above ▪ across ▪ around ▪ at ▪ behind ▪ below ▪ between ▪ beyond ▪
in ▪ in front of ▪ near ▪ next to ▪ on ▪ opposite

CARRIE'S VILLAGE

Carrie used to live _____¹ Number 7, Bow Road, very _____² the turn into Green Street. Going right from there, you soon come to the bus stop _____³ the village green. Then you come to the only shops in the village. Right _____⁴ the bus stop is the combined post office and newspaper shop, and two doors farther along is the general village store. _____⁵ them is the pub. The church and village hall are on the other side of the village green, and _____⁶ the hall, there is a small playground for children. Just _____⁷ the church is the churchyard, and _____⁸ that and the hall is the village sports ground.

   Coming back to the top of Bow Road, if you turn left there, the road soon divides into Sheep Street and Park Road. Not far down Sheep Street, there is a path _____⁹ a steep hill to the right of the road. That takes you up to the old castle _____¹⁰ the hill, high _____¹¹ the village, with wonderful views _____¹² miles of open country. Back down at the end of Sheep Street, you come to the Fish Hotel. Just _____¹³ the hotel is the River Wend, which is famous for its fishing. _____¹⁴ the grounds of the hotel there is a sports centre, where Carrie sometimes used to go to play tennis.

5 **GETTING IT RIGHT**

→ Simple past ▪ Past progressive, SB S. 251

Put the verbs in brackets in the simple past or past progressive.

Last year, three friends _____ [1] (live) together in a student house. However, they

_____ [2] (not get on) very well because no one _____ [3] (clean up)

after themselves. They _____ [4] (have) rules about the kitchen, but no one

_____ [5] (keep) to them. One evening they _____ [6] (all cook) at the

same time when they _____ [7] (have) a big argument. It _____ [8]

(start) when Ellie _____ [9] (look for) a pan – but they _____ [10] (be)

all dirty. Tim _____ [11] (try) to find some eggs, but when he _____ [12]

(open) the fridge, he quickly _____ [13] (have to) shut it again because of the smell. Jamie

_____ [14] (look forward) to some soup, but when he _____ [15] (look)

in the cupboard it _____ [16] (be) all gone. At first they all _____ [17]

(shout) at each other, but then they _____ [18] (agree) to change their ways.

6 **BUILDING SKILLS**

→ Rezeption: Hörverstehen, SB S. 225

🔘
7

Listen to Carrie's interview with the benefits officer and complete his notes.

PERSONAL DETAILS

Family name: _____ [1]   First name(s): _____ [2]

Age: _____ [3]   Date of birth: _____ [4]

Address: _____ [5]

Post code: _____ [6]   Telephone (mobile): _____ [7]

BUSINESS OPTIONS

Look at the graphic and then answer the questions. → Statistiken beschreiben, SB S. 238

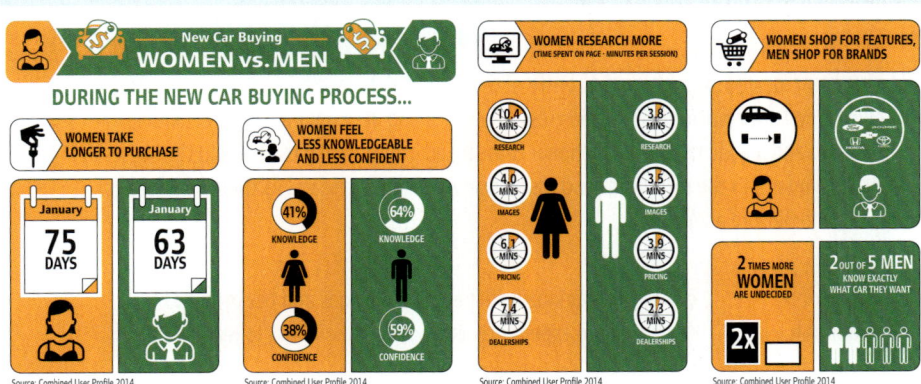

1   What could the reason be for the difference between men and women described in the infographic?
2   Look at the graphic about knowledge and confidence. Do you think it is true? Or is it just how the people feel?
3   Does this graphic describe you? Explain why or why not.
4   If you wanted to create a car advertisement, how could you use this information to model the advert?

1 LISTENING

→ Rezeption: Hörverstehen, SB S. 225

A careers advisor at the National Careers Service is helping two students to choose a suitable career. Listen to the two dialogues and fill in as much of the table as possible.

	Meera	Christopher
Age	_____ 1	_____ 8
Dream job	_____ 2	_____ 9
Free time activities	_____ 3	_____ 10
Favourite subject(s)	_____ 4	_____ 11
Least favourite subject(s)	_____ 5	_____ 12
Work experience	_____ 6	_____ 13
Recommendation	_____ 7	_____ 14

2 LOOKING AT THE TEXT

→ Rezeption: Leseverstehen, SB S. 214

RETAIL JOB SEARCH FORUM
Europe's top recruitment agency

5
Employer: Winter Adventure Centre
Location: Muonio, Northern Finland
Job title: Temporary waiter/waitress
Dates: September – March
Working hours: Minimum 40hrs per week incl. weekend work (Saturdays and Sundays), one month minimum
Pay: €1,000 per month + tips + overtime
10
Benefits: Free board and lodging in cottage in hotel complex Travel allowance of up to €300 for airfare to and from home country

Äkäskero is a small hotel and restaurant located 20km from the centre of the beautiful Pallas-Yllästunturi National Park, where husky safaris, snowmobiling, snowshoeing, ice fishing and cross-country skiing are popular winter activities.
15
We offer comfortable accommodation and a wide range of traditional Finnish and international cuisine and the successful candidate will be expected to wait on guests in the restaurant and assist elsewhere, as necessary. As there is no public transport, hotel vehicles can be used for leisure activities.

The successful candidate ...
◊ is polite, friendly, helpful and flexible   ◊ enjoys working with people of all ages and backgrounds
20
◊ speaks good English and/or German   ◊ has some experience as a waiter or is willing to learn

Have we described you? If so, send your application to Ms Laurukka Mäkelä, Director of Human Resources, through this website and we'll be in touch.

 UPLOAD CV    UPLOAD COVER LETTER

A Use the information in the advertisement to make notes on the following categories:

1 Length of contract   3 Accommodation   5 Insurance
2 Allowance   4 Food   6 Travel expenses

B   Match the words in the box with the definitions below.

waiter/waitress ▪ tip ▪ located ▪ range ▪ leisure ▪ experience ▪ willing ▪ application

1   CV and cover letter
2   free time
3   knowledge or skill gained from doing something
4   money given for good service, e.g. in a restaurant or hotel

5   person who serves guests in a restaurant
6   prepared or ready to do something
7   situated
8   variety

3   BUILDING SKILLS

→ Schriftliche Mediation, SB S. 240

Sie sollen einen Blogbeitrag über „Ferienjobs im Ausland" für die Homepage Ihrer Schule schreiben. Lesen Sie zuerst die *Skills checklist* über schriftliche Mediation durch, und schreiben Sie dann einen Beitrag, in dem Sie die wichtigsten Vor- und Nachteile des Jobs am *Winter Adventure Centre* in Finnland (Übung 2) beschreiben. Erklären Sie auch, ob Sie die Stelle empfehlen würden oder nicht.

SKILLS CHECKLIST: Written mediation

☑ Have I read the situation and instructions carefully?
☑ Have I read through the text and marked relevant information?
☑ Have I written the right sort of text?

4   WORKING WITH WORDS

Use words from the box to complete the letter from a company director to his employees explaining why they now need to hot-desk. Two words will be left over.

by default ▪ challenge ▪ downsize ▪ dress down ▪ filing cabinet ▪ gradual ▪ Human Resources ▪ property ▪ requires ▪ workforce

Dear colleagues,

I am sure you have all noticed the _____¹ changes that are happening around us. Five years ago we had a _____² of 350. Now the total number of employees is 575. In simple terms, our company is becoming too big for the building we are in.

So what can we do to deal with this _____³? One answer would be to _____⁴ the company, but making it smaller would mean job losses. Another would be to look for a bigger building, but the price of _____⁵ in our area is far too high.

Research has shown that not every employee _____⁶ a desk every day, and some desks are even empty four days a week. We therefore intend to introduce hot-desking, which is when every employee has a _____⁷ on wheels but no fixed desk. The new system will be demonstrated by the director of the _____⁸ department next Monday at 10 am. We hope you will attend this very important meeting and look forward to your co-operation.

Wallace Baxter
Managing Director

5 GETTING IT RIGHT

→ *If* sentences, SB S. 264

A Use the right form of the verbs in brackets (*if* sentences type 1) to complete the dialogue between a student and his mother.

Mother Have you seen this brochure about jobs, Nicholas? It says you _____¹ (not have) much chance of finding a good job if you _____² (not apply) early.

Student But not this early! If I _____³ (send) an employer an application now, they _____ _____⁴ (tell) me to apply next year.

Mother But if you _____⁵ (contact) them this year, they _____⁶ (put) you on their waiting list, Nicholas! What's wrong with that?

Student It's stupid. If I _____⁷ (change) my mind, I _____⁸ (be) on the wrong waiting list.

Mother Well, I know from experience that you _____⁹ (not find) anything if you _____¹⁰ (wait) too long.

B Use the right form of the verbs in brackets (*if* sentences type 2) to complete the telephone conversation between Angela Jolly, a secretary at ICL computer services, and her friend Ramona, who is a school secretary.

Ramona Hi Angie! How are things?

Angela Could be better. I think I _____¹ (be) a lot happier if I _____² (have) a job like yours.

Ramona Well, if you _____³ (work) here, you _____⁴ (deal) with hundreds of people every week. Sometimes it's very stressful.

Angela Well, I'm at home alone all day working on the phone and the computer. It _____⁵ (be) wonderful if I _____⁶ (see) people every day! I think I _____ _____⁷ (accept) a pay cut if it _____⁸ (mean) seeing more people again.

Ramona I see what you mean. _____⁹ (you / take) a part-time job at a school if one _____¹⁰ (come) up? I could do with some help here.

Angela Yes! That sounds absolutely marvellous!

6 BUILDING SKILLS

→ Produktion: Eine Stellungnahme schreiben, S. 234

A Use the expressions in the box to fill in the gaps in the comment about young people moving away from home for work. You can look at the *Language for writing* on the back flap of the student's book if you need help.

> another point to consider is this ▪ as a consequence ▪ firstly ▪ in my opinion ▪ to conclude ▪ on the other hand ▪ on the whole ▪ secondly ▪ there are several questions to think about when discussing ▪ on the one hand

SKILLS CHECKLIST: Writing a comment

- ☑ Have I read the statement carefully und understood it?
- ☑ Have I structured my arguments logically, e.g. with a mind map or under headings?
- ☑ Have I included arguments for and against?
- ☑ Have I referred to the topic in my first sentence and stated my opinion in the conclusion?

_____ ¹

the problems faced by young people when they move away from home. The first question is, how much do they really need their family, and the second is, what must they do to become truly independent?

_____², the family should give maximum support to a young person starting their first real job after school or college, _____³, because it is a very important moment in their life, _____⁴, because they may face big problems they can't solve alone and finally, because friends come and go but families are for life.

_____⁵ is it realistic in today's modern world to expect to find a job close to where you grew up and went to school? _____⁶ parents expect their children to be nearby to help them in their old age, but _____⁷ they want them to be independent, which often means being prepared to live and work a long way from home. _____⁸, the young person can easily feel guilty whatever they do.

_____⁹, I believe it's better to give young people the freedom to do what they want and be ready to help when things go wrong. _____¹⁰, I would say that help from the family is important at the beginning but less so as the young person becomes more and more independent.

B **Study the _Skills checklist_ then write a comment expressing your personal opinion about the following statement: 'People who work long hours and never take a break just make other people suffer. Work isn't the only thing in life.'**

Complete the text with the correct words from the box. The words are all from page 74 of the student's book.

male • equal • founders • conclusion • ratio • aim • females • quotas

I work as an investment banker, which is a profession with very few women. When I first started working at my company, I was one of only three _____¹ in my quite large department. Last year, one of the _____² of the company decided he wanted to do something about the _____³ of men to women. Instead of _____⁴, he decided to create a work environment which would _____⁵ to encourage women to apply to our company. For example, he decided that _____⁶ pay for all employees was a must. He also drew the _____⁷ that a lot of women don't go into banking because of the long hours, which are not family friendly, so he decided to make working from home easier. Not only did this increase the number of women working for the company, it created a lot of happy _____⁸ employees, who were also able to enjoy the new benefits.

1 BUILDING SKILLS

→ Gründliches Lesen, SB S. 223

A Read the questions and underline words that may help you to find the relevant areas of the text.

1 What sort of ethnic community did Benjamin Zephaniah grow up in?
2 What went wrong with his education?
3 What did the BBC poll show?
4 Why might we be surprised by this?
5 Why did he refuse the offer of the OBE?

> **SKILLS CHECKLIST:**
> **Reading for understanding**
>
> ☑ Have I looked for key words in the questions?
> ☑ Have I found the key words in the text?
> ☑ Have I compared my answers with the questions and the text?

B Read the text and underline key words that help to provide the answers.

BENJAMIN OBADIAH IQBAL ZEPHANIAH:

British poet, story-teller and song-writer

Born in Britain in 1958. His parents were both from the Caribbean islands, and he grew up in Handsworth, Birmingham – an area he calls 'the Jamaican capital of Europe'. He left school at 13, unable to read or write. But with Jamaican music and poetry in his blood and angry street politics on his mind, he had a lot to say. He said it through public
5 performances of his hard-hitting poems. By the age of 15, he had *made a big name for himself* across Handsworth's large Jamaican and wider Afro-Caribbean community.

He did not fit well into the British social structure, and as a young man he was in trouble with the law and spent time in *prison*. Nor did his *anti-Establishment* ideas fit well, and over the years, he has continued his attacks on the Establishment. He has attacked, for
10 example, the British legal system, the monarchy, the political system, unfair treatment of minority groups in society and past *wrongdoings* of the British Empire.

Despite all this, he has also become one of Britain's most popular writers, and in a BBC poll he was voted the UK's third most-loved poet. He is Professor of Creative Writing at Brunel University, and his work is widely *recognized*.
15 However, he remains happily on the outside of society looking in. In 2003, for example, the Government offered him a medal, which he would receive from the Queen at Buckingham Palace. The medal was the OBE (short for The Order of the British Empire). His reply was immediate and clear though: 'Benjamin Zephaniah OBE – no way *Mr Blair*[1], no way Mrs Queen. I am *profoundly* anti-Empire.'

(264 words)

[1] Tony Blair, Prime Minister from 1997 to 2007

Benjamin Zephaniah performing in London in 2010

Vocabulary notes			
to make a name for yourself	*sich einen Namen machen*	wrongdoing	*Vergehen*
prison	*Gefängnis*	to recognize	*anerkennen*
anti-Establishment	*gegen das Establishment*	profoundly	*zutiefst*

C Write full answers to questions 1–5 in part A.

D Read your answers carefully and compare them to the questions to make sure that you have given the details required.

2 WORKING WITH WORDS

A Complete the table with words from the text in exercise 1.

Noun (person)	Noun (thing)	Noun (person)	Noun (thing)
performer	_____ 1	politician	_____ 3
poet	_____ / _____ 2	singer	_____ 4

B **Use pairs of words from A to complete the following.**

1 **A** Lucy is a good _____¹, and she plays the guitar well, too.

   B Yes, and did you know that she's recently started writing her own _____² as well.

2 **A** I don't like the way the _____³ are running this country!

   B Well, if you don't agree with them, you'll have to go into _____⁴ yourself and try to change things.

3 He is a great _____⁵, so the best way to experience his poetry is to go to one of his live _____⁶.

4 Benjamin Zephaniah has written a number of stories such as *Refugee Boy*, but he first became known as a _____⁷, and he is still most famous for his _____⁸, which are usually short, often angry, and often funny, too.

3 GETTING IT RIGHT

→ *If* sentences, SB S. 264

Form type 3 conditionals from the following sentence parts, adding words as necessary. Start each sentence with *if*.

GETTING BACK TO AUSTRALIA

When Tom Blake was young, his family visited Australia on holiday. He loved the country and as he grew up, he often wished he could go back and get to know it better. Years later, with unemployment very high in the UK as he left college, his thoughts turned to Australia again.

1 unemployment not be so high in Britain / Tom find work without much difficulty
   If unemployment had not been so high in Britain, Tom would have _____
   _____

2 get job in UK / stay Britain quite happily
   _____

3 things go well for him / not wonder about work in other countries
   _____

4 never be to Australia / be certain never think about working somewhere so far away
   _____
   _____

5 not look for work there though / miss perfect job for him – as tour guide for visitors
   _____
   _____

6 not take tour group up Gold Coast / never meet perfect girl for him, and champion surfer Jenny never become the love of his life!
   _____
   _____

4 GETTING IT RIGHT

→ Past perfect ▪ Simple past, SB S. 256

Put the verbs in brackets into the simple past or past perfect.

After Alem's father (go) _____ [1] back to East Africa, the authorities (give) _____ [2]

the teenager a new life in England – just as his father (expect) _____ [3]. Even though

Alem (never visit) _____ [4] England before, he soon (begin) _____ [5]

to feel comfortable with his new family, school and friends. It (be) _____ [6] much more pleasant than

the dangers he (experience) _____ [7] at home in East Africa with his parents.

But then, one day, Alem (receive) _____ [8] a letter from his father with terrible news of

what (happen) _____ [9] to his mother. He (learn) _____ [10] that she

(disappear) _____ [11] before his father's return from England. Then Alem (read)

_____ [12] the thing that he (be) _____ [13] most afraid of: his father's letter

(explain) _____ [14] how he (finally find) _____ [15]

her dead body near the border between Eritrea and Ethiopia.

5 LISTENING

→ Rezeption: Hörverstehen, SB S. 225

Listen and complete the table with the missing figures.

Source: *www.migrationpolicy.org*

Population of the USA from 1970–2012 (millions)			
Year	Total	*Immigrants	Percentage (approx)
1970	203.2	9.6	[3]
1980	226.5	[1]	6
1990	248.7	19.8	[4]
2000	281.4	[2]	11
2012	313.7	40.8	[5]

6 BUILDING SKILLS

→ Produktion: Statistiken beschreiben und analysieren, SB S. 238

A Study the table to complete the analysis by circling the right words in brackets.

Population of the USA from 1870–1970 (millions)			
Year	Total	Immigrants	Percentage
1870	38.6	5.8	14.9
1890	63.0	9.7	15.4
1910	92.2	14.0	15.2
1930	123.2	14.4	11.7
1950	151.3	10.4	6.9
1970	203.2	9.6	4.8

SKILLS Checklist: Analysing figures

☑ Have I read the labels carefully?
☑ Have I understood the units that the figures are presented in?

Between 1870 and 1910, US immigrant numbers (rose / fell)[1] from (under / over)[2] six million to (a little under / almost exactly)[3] fourteen million. At one point, their numbers (reached / fell to)[4] 15.4% of the country's total population. However, from then until 1930, there was (little change / no change)[5] in the immigrant population, while at the same time the total US population continued to (fall / increase)[6] (rapidly / slowly)[7] – from (around / exactly)[8] 92 million in 1910 to (approximately / exactly)[9] 123 million in 1930. This meant that as a percentage of the total, the trend was (downwards / upwards)[10] – from 15.2% to just 11.7%. This (rise / fall)[11] continued until 1970, when immigrants formed (less than / more than)[12] 5% of America's population.

B Use the table in exercise 5 to complete a further analysis. Add language offered in 6A.

After the long _____[1] in immigrant numbers as a percentage of the total population, the trend turned _____[2] after 1970, and numbers _____[3] _____[4]. So, by 2012, the immigrant population was _____[5] 40 million – _____[6] 13% of the total.

C Use the Internet to find the latest possible figures. Use them to continue the analysis. Begin like this:

Since 2012, the figures have risen again to levels that the country last saw over a century ago. The latest statistics show that _____

_____

_____

_____

_____

_____

A Make collocations by matching one word from box A with one word from box B.

A market • intercultural • set • shake • advertising • personal • eye • slang

B hands • words • space • campaign • competence • up • contact • share

_____   _____

_____   _____

_____   _____

B Now match the collocations with the definitions below.

1 vocabulary that is not always proper

_____

2 how people in some cultures greet each other

_____

3 this is important to have if you travel a lot

_____

4 in some cultures this is aggressive, in others it is polite

_____

5 the area around your body _____

6 found or start something _____

7 organized programme of adverts _____

8 amount a company sells compared to its competitors _____

1 WORKING WITH WORDS

Complete the word families using forms from the five texts on page 90 of the student's book.

Verb	Noun	Noun (person)	Adjective
to produce	production	_____ 1	productive
_____	_____ 2	_____	charitable
_____ 3	donation	_____ 4	_____
to complain	_____ 5	_____	_____
to sponsor	_____ 6	sponsor	_____
_____	_____ 7	accountant	_____
_____ 8	empowerment	_____	_____
to amaze	amazement	_____	_____ 9
to save	_____ 10	_____	safe
_____	_____ 11	companion	_____
_____	homelessness	_____	_____ 12

2 BUILDING SKILLS

→ Produktion: Schaubilder beschreiben und analysieren, SB S. 238

Foreign aid

In 1970 the world's richest countries promised to increase their annual aid budgets to 0.7% of gross national income (GNI). GNI means a country's income generated both inside and outside the country.

SKILLS CHECKLIST: Comparing figures in charts

- ☑ Have I pointed out the most striking features?
- ☑ Have I contrasted categories with each other?
- ☑ Have I described the relationships between the categories?

A Study the chart and say ...

1 which country is closest to reaching the 0.7% target. _____

2 which country is furthest from the target.

_____

3 which countries donate almost the same proportion of their GNI. _____

_____

4 which English-speaking country donates the highest percentage of its GNI.

_____

5 which country is in sixth place in the chart.

_____

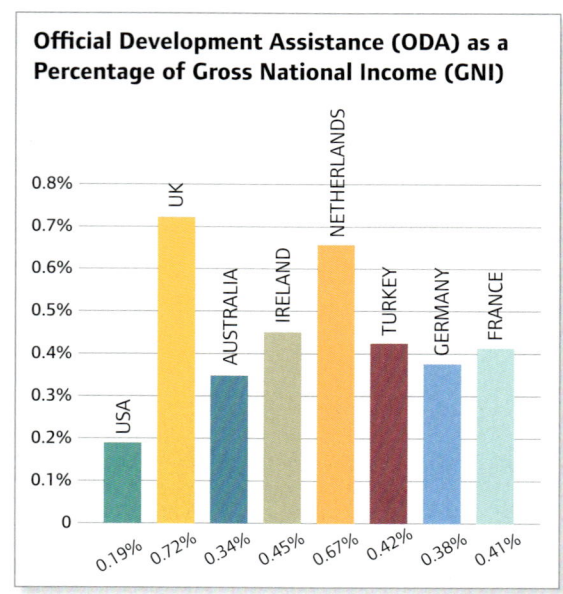

Official Development Assistance (ODA) as a Percentage of Gross National Income (GNI)

USA 0.19% UK 0.72% AUSTRALIA 0.34% IRELAND 0.45% NETHERLANDS 0.67% TURKEY 0.42% GERMANY 0.38% FRANCE 0.41%

B Use expressions from the *Building skills* box on page 92 and the *Useful phrases* on page 93 of the student's book to complete the text.

The chart shows the _____¹ of their GNI that rich countries spend on aid, and we can _____² see that there are big differences. The UK is in first _____³ while Germany only _____⁴ sixth, and the figure in the first _____⁵ shows us that the USA is last. The _____⁶ for Germany (0.38%) is exactly _____⁷ as much as for the USA (0.19%). Australia (0.34%) spends about _____⁸ as much on aid as the Netherlands (0.67%).

C Study the chart about individual giving on page 92 of the student's book and compare it with this chart about government giving. Write 4–5 sentences to show the differences.

Begin like this: *Whereas private American individuals donate most money to help others, their government ...*

3 LOOKING AT THE TEXTS

→ Rezeption: Leseverstehen, SB S. 214

A Read the texts on page 94 of the student's book and say if the following statements are true (T), false (F) or not in the text (N). Correct the false statements.

1	Kevin and Sandra Forkan were in Sri Lanka with four of their children.	☐
2	The children who survived were near the British Embassy.	☐
3	The British Embassy gave them a lot of help.	☐
4	The Forkan children were strong because their parents taught them to think of themselves first.	☐
5	The two brothers learned a lot about business when they travelled the world separately.	☐
6	They founded a flip-flop company in India with Mahatma Gandhi.	☐
7	The Gandys Foundation is a company which makes flip-flops.	☐
8	Paul and Rob Forkan plan to open more than one children's home.	☐

B Can you find the words hidden in the anagrams below? The answers are all in the *Orphans for Orphans* text on page 94 of the student's book.

1 LNBIGSSI ☐☐☐☐☐☐☐☐

2 EAIDCV ☐☐☐☐☐☐

3 TIHKHEIDCH ☐☐☐☐☐☐☐☐☐☐

4 ETTGNRHS ☐☐☐☐☐☐☐☐

5 RTAAIHINNMAU ☐☐☐☐☐☐☐☐☐☐☐☐

6 SEAPAOHRGN ☐☐☐☐☐☐☐☐☐☐

7 RLIVUVAS ☐☐☐☐☐☐☐☐

8 IYRCHAT ☐☐☐☐☐☐☐

4 LISTENING

→ Rezeption: Hörverstehen, SB S. 225

Listen to the podcast about the work of *Rebuilding Sri Lanka*, a charity set up after the tsunami in 2004 and complete the sentences with a, b or c.

Vocabulary notes	
to borrow a book	ein Buch ausleihen
to lend a book	jdm. ein Buch leihen

1 The tsunami
  a destroyed Clare Allen's hotel.
  b didn't destroy Clare Allen's hotel.
  c killed Clare Allen's daughter.

2 After the tsunami
  a a million Sri Lankans were homeless.
  b a million Sri Lankans were left dead.
  c 40,000 Sri Lankans were homeless.

3 The *Rebuilding Sri Lanka* charity
  a plans to build five libraries.
  b is building five libraries.
  c has built five libraries.

4 Schoolchildren who wish to pass their school-leaving exams
  a can borrow books from the *Rebuilding Sri Lanka* charity's libraries.
  b receive £2,000 from the *Rebuilding Sri Lanka* charity.
  c receive extra lessons from the *Rebuilding Sri Lanka* charity.

5 The *Rebuilding Sri Lanka* charity has a library which
  a lends out 2,700 books every Saturday.
  b lends out more than 200 books every Saturday.
  c is closed to its 2,700 members on Saturday.

6 The *Rebuilding Sri Lanka* charity
  a provides schoolchildren with cheap meals at school.
  b encourages children to go to school by giving them free food.
  c teaches schoolchildren to cook their own food at school.

7 The *Rebuilding Sri Lanka* charity has a centre
  a for traumatized children.
  b for traumatized parents.
  c where counsellors can receive training.

8 Most of the money donated to the *Rebuilding Sri Lanka* charity is spent on
  a administration.
  b its website design.
  c people in need.

5 GETTING IT RIGHT

→ Present perfect ▪ Present perfect progressive, SB S. 253

A **Write the present perfect forms of the verbs in the table.**

Verb	Simple statement	Question	Negative
1 to ask (I)	I've ... ⁱ1	Have I ... 2	3
2 to drive (you)	4	5	6
3 to fall (she)	7	8	9
4 to feel (we)	10	11	12
5 to wear (they)	13	14	15

B Now write the present perfect progressive forms of the same verbs in the table.

Verb	Simple statement	Question	Negative
1 to ask (I)	_____ 1	_____ 2	_____ 3
2 to drive (you)	_____ 4	_____ 5	_____ 6
3 to fall (she)	_____ 7	_____ 8	_____ 9
4 to feel (we)	_____ 10	_____ 11	_____ 12
5 to wear (they)	_____ 13	_____ 14	_____ 15

C Complete the sentences with the present perfect or the present perfect progressive. Use the present perfect progressive when possible.

1 Rob and Paul Forkan _____ (write) a book called *Tsunami Kids*.

2 They _____ (sell) thousands of copies already.

3 The two brothers _____ (sell) Gandys flip-flops since 2012.

4 Katy Brown is a bookshop assistant and _____ (wear) her Gandys

for eight hours, since she started work this morning.

5 She _____ (buy) two pairs of Gandys flip-flops.

6 So far this year Katy _____ (donate) £25 to charity.

7 Her shop _____ (start) to collect money for good causes.

8 She _____ (work) at the shop for two months now.

9 She _____ (serve) customers since 9 o'clock this morning.

10 Nine customers _____ (buy) a copy of *Tsunami Kids* today.

Look at the text on page 98 of the student's book and choose the correct answer to the following questions.   → Rezeption: Leseverstehen, SB S. 214

1 **What makes FINCA different from other banks?**
   ☐ **A** They loan large amounts of money to people who want to start new companies.
   ☐ **B** They loan small amounts of money to people who have a hard time getting loans.
   ☐ **C** They loan money to anyone who needs it.

2 **Why do people criticize microfinance?**
   ☐ **A** Microfinance doesn't solve the big problem of world poverty.
   ☐ **B** Nobody benefits from microfinance.
   ☐ **C** The interest rates for microfinance are very high.

3 **Who is Nelson Lopez?**
   ☐ **A** He rents a small citrus farm from FINCA.
   ☐ **B** He lent $10,000 to a farmer.
   ☐ **C** He owns a small citrus farm and borrowed money from FINCA to keep it running.

11 Global reach

1 WORKING WITH WORDS

A Match these nouns from the text on page 100 of the student's book to the verb-noun pairs below.

action ▪ contact ▪ a contract ▪ an order ▪ quality

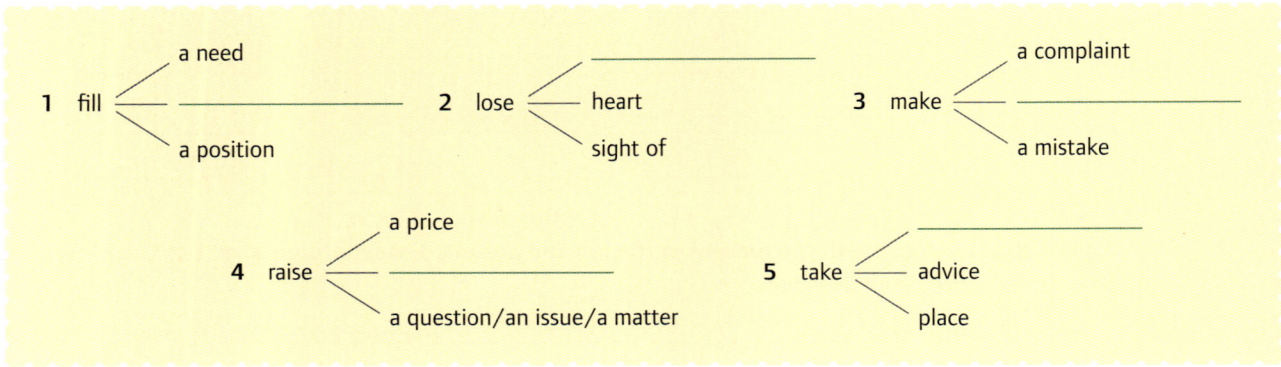

1 fill ⟨ a need / _____ / a position

2 lose ⟨ _____ / heart / sight of

3 make ⟨ a complaint / _____ / a mistake

4 raise ⟨ a price / _____ / a question/an issue/a matter

5 take ⟨ _____ / advice / place

B Replace the words in brackets with verb-noun pairs from part A. Make any changes necessary.

1 I think I've (got something wrong) _____ with these figures. They don't match the figures on the bill.

2 The Sunrise is a cheap, reliable car that (provides something necessary) _____ in the Indian market.

3 We've agreed that the next union meeting will (happen) _____ at 8 pm on Friday, 10 March.

4 When Tony became unemployed, he tried hard to find a new job, but slowly he (stopped hoping) _____ .

5 Before the company decides to build the new factory, I'd like to (ask something) _____ _____ about costs.

6 **A** I'd like to apply for the job of export manager that you were advertising recently.

   B I'm afraid you're too late. We've already (chosen someone for that job) _____ .

7 I'm sorry, but I need to (tell you that I'm not happy) _____ about the equipment that you sold us: it's not working properly.

8 I'm worried about this contract. Before we sign it, I think we should (ask somebody to advise us) _____ .

9 As western companies look for cheaper sources of supply in SE Asia, they often (forget) _____ the fact that working conditions can be terrible in places like Bangladesh.

10 All our products are too cheap! We have to (increase the amount that we ask people to pay us) _____ , or we won't be able to stay in business for much longer!

2 GETTING IT RIGHT

→ The passive, SB S. 261

A Use the simple present passive to describe a process. Add '*by* + agent' if necessary.

1 Farmers from all over the Gumutindo district grow coffee organically.

   Coffee is _____

2 Then they bring the coffee to the new central production facility.

   _____

3 There, highly-trained senior staff check quality and quantity.

   _____

4 Then workers process the raw coffee in carefully-controlled conditions.

   _____

5 After that, the Cooperative's new, automated equipment packs the coffee.

   _____

6 Finally, they send the finished product to Mombasa for export to Europe and America.

   _____

B Turn Steve Race's spoken comments into part of the journalist's formal report. Put the underlined comments into the correct passive tenses. Add '*by* + agent' if necessary.

So it's finally happened – and I'm angry. The company owners up in New York have closed the factory here in Virginia, and they've thrown 200 workers out of our jobs. I hear they made the decision last summer, but they didn't tell the workforce till last month. It seems they'll send all the equipment from the Virginia plant to a new factory in Indonesia, and people there will produce the same furniture for a quarter of the pay.

But when they move production offshore like this, it exports American jobs, too, and that damages the American economy. Don't these New York money men understand? It's crazy! If we close every US factory, we will completely destroy the US economy. Then who will buy all those 'made in Asia' products?

200 JOBS LOST AT ACE FURNITURE
The ACE FURNITURE factory here in Virginia

_____
_____
_____
_____
_____
_____
_____
_____
_____

3 BUILDING SKILLS

→ Produktion: Cartoons beschreiben und analysieren, SB S. 236

Follow these steps to write a cartoon analysis:

1 Describe the cartoon.
2 Explain this ironic comment on the effects of globalization.
3 Use the newspaper headlines to explain further.
4 Comment on the manager's words in the cartoon.
5 Say what the cartoonist is attacking here.

> **SKILLS CHECKLIST: Describing cartoons**
>
> ☑ Have I read the caption(s) or speech bubble(s)?
> ☑ Have I described everything in the cartoon?
> ☑ Have I used the present progressive to describe what is happening?

DEVELOPED ECONOMIES NOT COMPETITIVE WITH FAR EAST

MANY US AND EUROPEAN JOBS EXPORTED TO DEVELOPING WORLD

UNCERTAIN FUTURE FOR WESTERN WORKERS

This cartoon shows _____

_____

_____

_____

_____

_____

_____

WE'RE GOING TO HAVE TO LET YOU GO...WE'VE FOUND SOMEONE IN CHINA WHO IS 45% BETTER AT BEING YOU FOR 24% LESS

4 LISTENING

→ Rezeption: Hörverstehen, SB S. 225

A Listen to the Twin Trading field officer's report on Gumutindo Cooperative's coffee sales. Complete the column 'Changes in production'.

Period		Changes in production (kilos)	Description of changes
Year 1	1st half	*0–500*	*rose gradually*
	2nd half	_____ 1	_____ 8
Year 2	1st half	_____ 2	_____ 9
	2nd half	_____ 3	_____ 10
Year 3	1st half	_____ 4	_____ 11
	2nd half	_____ 5	_____ 12
Year 4	1st half	_____ 6	_____ 13
	2nd half	_____ 7	_____ 14

B Listen again, this time for the way the changes are described. Complete the column 'Description of changes'.

5 **BUILDING SKILLS**   → Produktion: Schaubilder beschreiben und analysieren, SB S. 238

A Use the information from the table to complete the chart.

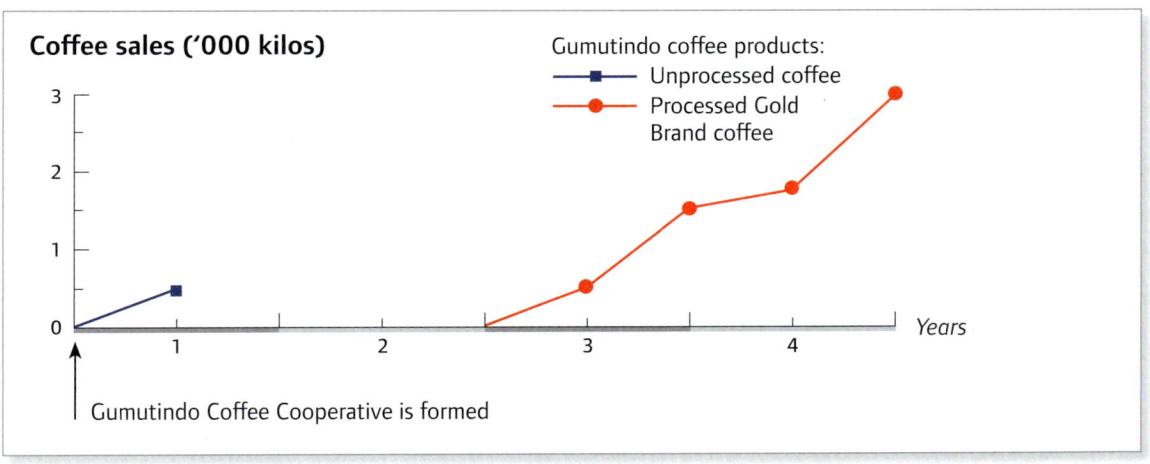

B Now describe sales of Gumutindo Gold Brand coffee. Start like this:

Gumutindo Gold Brand
In the first half of Year 3, sales _____ from _____ to …

Complete the crossword with words from page 108 of the student's book.

ACROSS
4 something difficult or worrying that gives you a hard time
6 suffering or death caused by lack of food
9 a religious person who celebrates Christmas

DOWN
1 a person whose religion began in India
2 a place that protects you from weather
3 the houses or shelter that people live in
5 the state of being able to read or write
7 with a name that is not known
8 to get better

1 WORKING WITH WORDS

A Match words from box 1 with words from box 2 to form word pairs from the text on pages 110 and 111 of the student's book.

1
> daytime ▪ entry-level ▪ job ▪ middle ▪ minimum ▪ pay ▪ production ▪ retail ▪ university ▪ welfare

2
> application ▪ assistant ▪ degree ▪ industry ▪ job ▪ management ▪ packet ▪ system ▪ TV ▪ wage

B Use word pairs from A to complete the following sentences.

1 A lot of people don't earn enough to be able to support their families properly. The government needs to raise the _____ .

2 The _____ is very competitive. Look at the fierce competition between supermarkets, for example.

3 Tessa has always been interested in producing books and magazines, and now she's started work as a _____ with a big publisher.

4 Ralph was a junior manager for several years, but now he has risen to a job in _____ _____ .

5 Before the modern _____ was introduced, there was little to protect the poor, the elderly and the sick, apart from family, friends and charity.

6 I'm applying for an _____ job, so it isn't very well paid, but it's a good start.

7 Carla will have to study for another four years if she wants to get a _____ _____ .

8 It's very hard to find work at the moment. I've sent out hundreds of _____ , but I've only been offered two interviews so far.

9 Tony isn't doing much about finding a job. He just sits at home and watches _____ all day long!

10 I'm tired of being poor! It would be great if I could find a full-time job and get a proper _____ _____ every month.

2 GETTING IT RIGHT

→ Modal verbs, SB S. 259

A Complete a reporter's interview with the publisher of the online publication *Business Now* by circling the right modal verbs in brackets.

Reporter Is it true that you don't usually pay your contributors?

Publisher That's right. In general, I find that we (needn't / mustn't)¹ pay because people want to give us their material anyway.

Reporter But is that right? It seems to me that you really (should / might)² pay. I mean, how (might / can)³ writers go on writing if publishers don't pay them?

Publisher Well, most people who write for *Business Now* (can't / don't have to)⁴ make money from it because they have other jobs.

Reporter	Yes, but your publication is a business like any other, and it seems to me that every business (must / may)[5] pay its suppliers properly – or else it isn't a real business.
Publisher	No, no, you (needn't / shouldn't)[6] think about it like that. You see, *Business Now* doesn't make big profits, so we simply (can't / mustn't)[7] pay much. And remember this, we (have to / may)[8] deal with many other costs, so free contributions help us to survive.
Reporter	So why do people do it?
Publisher	For various reasons, I think. For example, people (should / may)[9] write for *Business Now* because they want to share their ideas and help others in similar situations. There are others who (might / can't)[10] do it just to make a name for themselves in their own organizations.

B Complete the dialogues. Use *can/can't* or *could/couldn't* when possible. When necessary, use forms of *(not) be able to*.

1 A Have you prepared your new CV yet?

B I _____[1] yet, but I _____[2] have it ready by tomorrow.

2 A How did you get on at your interview?

B Well, I _____[1] see that they were quite interested in me, but I

_____[2] be sure that they were ready to offer me the job.

3 A What about the general test that the company asks all candidates to do? A lot of people

_____[1] finish in the time that they allow.

B Yes, that went all right, I think, and I _____[2] answer all the questions.

4 A Well done for getting the job! But I hear that they wanted you to start on Monday, so why aren't you at work now?

B I _____[1] start straight away because I had to go away. But I told them and

luckily, I _____[2] change the start date to next Monday.

---

3 **LISTENING**

→ Rezeption: Hörverstehen, SB S. 225

A Listen to Brazilian student Carlos use Skype to talk to someone at Windsor Park Retirement Home. Take notes about the resident for him.

> Name: _____ Age: _____ Years at WPRH: _____
>
> Family:
>   Wife: _____
>   Children/ages: _____
>   Grandchildren/ages: _____
> Interests: 1 _____ 2 _____ 3 _____

B Listen again and decide whether these statements are true (T) or false (F).

1	This is the first time that Carlos has talked to this elderly American.	☐
2	This person lived on his own for twelve years after his wife died.	☐
3	He moved to Windsor Park Retirement Home because he was lonely.	☐

4 His sons both have families, but not his daughter. ☐

5 His whole family gave him a surprise birthday party yesterday. ☐

6 They used the restaurant at Windsor Park. ☐

7 He enjoys various activities at Windsor Park, but he seems to enjoy going out even more. ☐

C Now correct the false statements.

_____

_____

_____

_____

4 GETTING IT RIGHT
→ The passive, SB S. 261

Rewrite the Mill Hill Retirement Home's rules more formally. Use passive modal forms.

RULES FOR VISITORS

1 Whenever possible, you should plan visits for normal visiting hours. (However, we may allow visits at other times by special arrangement.)

_____

_____

2 Please note that sometimes we may not allow a visit if a resident is very unwell.

_____

3 Visitors must sign in at reception.

_____

4 We are sorry, but you cannot bring pets into the building.

_____

5 You are welcome to eat with us, and you can order visitors' meals by phone or email 24 hours in advance.

_____

_____

6 All communication with staff is very welcome, but you should not interrupt nurses when preparing residents' medications.

_____

_____

5 BUILDING SKILLS
→ Ein Wörterbuch benutzen, SB S. 217

Read the dictionary definitions (1–6) and match them to sentences a–f below.

work /wɜːk/ verb [I or T]   **1** to do a job, especially the job you do to make money   **2** If a machine works, it operates correctly.   **3** If you work a machine, you make it operate.   **4** to be effective, to go according to plan   **5** to arrange for something to happen, especially by doing it secretly and cleverly   **6** to shape, change or process a substance

FOUNDATION COURSE

Unit 1 The cult of celebrity

1 TALKING ABOUT CELEBRITY

fans, paparazzi, famous, status, star, luxury, legend, stalker, actor, image, autograph, popularity

2 GETTING IT RIGHT

1 A, 2 A, 3 B, 4 A, 5 B, 6 A, 7 A, 8 B

3 GETTING IT RIGHT

1	are	9	am scared
2	love	10	tells
3	have	11	come
4	enter	12	smiles
5	sees	13	relax
6	is not happy	14	says
7	is	15	feels
8	asks	16	win

4 ASKING QUESTIONS

1	What is/What's	4	Why are
2	Where are	5	When do
3	How do	6	Who is

5 BUILDING SKILLS
b

6 LOOKING AT THE TEXT

1 False. Desirée is last month's winner of *Stars for Tomorrow*.
2 False. Patrick is one of the judges on *Stars for Tomorrow*. (He and Desirée are in a relationship.)
3 True
4 False. She accepts that paparazzi take photos when she is not looking perfect / having a bad day.
5 False. The media is full of reports about her personal life.
6 True

7 GETTING IT RIGHT

1	am calling	6	are going too far
2	are you doing	7	Are they trying
3	am reading	8	are only doing
4	is the press making up	9	are walking up
5	are dating	10	am driving into

8 GETTING IT RIGHT

1	am working	5	are looking
2	is going	6	know
3	am having	7	believe
4	stalk	8	love

Unit 2 The world of sport

1 TALKING ABOUT SPORT

	A		B
1	participant	1	keep-fit activities
2	spectator	2	do aerobics
3	football	3	go jogging
4	play tennis	4	participant
5	support a team	5	football
6	keep-fit activities	6	spectator
7	do aerobics		
8	go jogging		

2 GETTING IT RIGHT

1	went	4	began
2	played	5	bought
3	won	6	took part

3 GETTING IT RIGHT

A
1 1 has left; 2 has just moved (signal word: just)
2 1 has not arrived; 2 has never been (signal words: yet, never)
3 1 Have you heard; 2 has just joined (signal words: already, just)
4 1 Have you met; 2 has played (signal word: yet)

B

1	for	5	since
2	for	6	since
3	since	7	since
4	for	8	for

4 GETTING IT RIGHT

1 charged (earlier today)
2 has not said (up till now)
3 searched (earlier this week)
4 has won (during his career)
5 told (yesterday)
6 drank (before)
7 has sponsored (for)
8 said (this morning)
9 has been (for)
10 gave (before)
11 were (as always)
12 have ever contained (ever)

5 GETTING IT RIGHT

A
1 him
2 me
3 **1** She; **2** them
4 **1** us; **2** it
5 **1** They; **2** We; **3** it

B
9 subject pronouns (sp); 9 object pronouns (op);
6 possessive adjectives (pa)

line 1 my (pa); We (sp)
line 2 Her (op); She (sp)
line 3 It (sp)
line 4 us (op)
line 5 his (pa); Its (pa)
line 6 him (op); me (op); you (sp)
line 7 I (sp); him (op); he (sp); me (op); It (sp)
line 8 we (sp); His (pa); us (op); them (op)
line 9 their (pa); They (sp)
line 10 you (sp); me (op); your (pa)

6 BUILDING SKILLS

A/B
Expressions we hear: 1, 3, 4, 5, 6, 8, 9
Expressions we don't hear: 2, 7

C
Jane:
1 does aerobics
2 home
3 heart, lungs
4 stress
5 (too) expensive

Will:
1 goes swimming
2 at local swimming pool
3 work-out
4 sleep well
5 weight
6 slim and stay slim

Lily:
1 plays volleyball
2 at college
3 lose
4 burns up
5 friends
6 get to know people
7 good friends

Unit 3 Fashion and brand power

1 TALKING ABOUT BRANDS

A
1 slogan
2 fashionable
3 price
4 product
5 affordable
6 quality
7 advertising
8 values
9 choice
10 famous

B
brand names

2 GETTING IT RIGHT

A
1 carefully
2 simply
3 beautiful
4 usually
5 similar
6 expensive; cheaply

B
1 Lucy <u>frequently</u> shops at the outlet store.
2 Jim <u>always</u> dresses well.
3 My new computer <u>suddenly</u> stopped working. /
<u>Suddenly</u> my new computer stopped working.
4 The coffee in that café is <u>usually</u> good.
5 I <u>really</u> want these boots.

3 USING A DICTIONARY
1 choose
2 choosy
3 cost
4 costly
5 affordability
6 afford

4 GETTING IT RIGHT

A/B
1 bigger than
2 biggest
3 lighter than
4 as heavy as
5 heavier than
6 as long as
7 longest
8 cheapest
9 more expensive than
10 most expensive
11 best
12 most difficult

C
The NeatPhone because it's the lightest and it looks
the nicest.

5 COLLOCATIONS
1 low
2 victim
3 new
4 copies
5 house

6 BUILDING SKILLS

A
(Lösungsvorschläge)

Giving an opinion	(Personally,) I think / feel / believe (that) … It seems to me (that) … If you ask me, … My (own) view of the matter / problem is …
Giving reasons	You see, … The reason is (simply) (that) … The main / basic reason is (that) … The thing is, you see, …
Agreeing with an opinion	Yes, I agree. (Absolutely.) That's (quite) right / true. I couldn't agree more. Yes, that's just how I see it. That's exactly my own view / opinion …
Disagreeing with an opinion	I don't agree. (Well,) as a matter of fact, … Actually, / In fact, I think (that) … (I'm afraid) I can't accept that.
Interrupting	I'm sorry to interrupt / break in, but … Excuse me for interrupting / breaking in, but … Can I (just) stop / interrupt you there for a moment?

B

1	view	3	reason	5	afraid
2	opinion	4	disagree	6	interrupt / believe

C–E

(freie Lösungen)

Unit 4 Leisure and free time

1 TALKING ABOUT FREE TIME ACTIVITIES

(freie Lösung)

2 GETTING IT RIGHT

A

1	Will you come	5	Will I see
2	will probably be	6	won't have
3	won't be	7	will help
4	will cancel	8	will be able to

B

1 I am going to train for the next marathon.
2 Mark and Mindy are going to go backpacking in Australia next summer.
3 Some pupils are going to start a film club next term.
4 The snooker championships are going to be held in Paris this year.
5 Are you really going to buy a motorbike?
6 I'm not going to go shopping for the rest of the year.

3 BUILDING SKILLS

A

1	is lying	4	are watching	7	is standing
2	is	5	hungrily	8	angry
3	is looking	6	are flying	9	is shouting

B

b

4 LOOKING AT THE TEXT

1 F, 2 F, 3 F, 4 T, 5 F, 6 T

5 BUILDING SKILLS

(Lösungsvorschlag)

Hallo …

Tut mir leid, dass du wieder Stress mit deiner Mutter hast! Ich habe kürzlich in einem Blog gelesen, dass uns allen ständig gesagt wird: „Als ich in deinem Alter war …!" Wie wahr! Die Leute, die das sagen, wissen echt, wie sie einem den Tag ruinieren …

Was diese Leute nicht verstehen, ist, dass heute eben nicht gestern ist! Wir machen ja immer noch total viel mit unseren Freunden, aber wir machen es eben anders – im Netz. Naja, ok, das ist dann nicht so direkt von Angesicht zu Angesicht, aber wir kommunizieren ja genauso viel, machen gemeinsam Hausaufgaben, tauschen Ideen aus usw. Und dabei lernen wir die ganze Zeit auch immer wieder neue Leute kennen!

Warum können ältere Leute nicht mal akzeptieren, dass sich die Welt weiter dreht und verändert? Und vielleicht sollten sie ab und zu mal darüber nachdenken, dass sie auch mal jung waren …

6 GETTING IT RIGHT

1	any	6	many	11	many
2	much	7	any	12	many
3	little	8	many	13	a few
4	a few	9	a little	14	much
5	some	10	some		

7 BUILDING SKILLS

(Lösungsvorschlag)

The photo shows a girl dressed in summer clothes, sitting on a platform next to a railway track. The tracks are in the countryside and are leading to a forest. The girl is alone, and she has a backpack and a sleeping mat with her. She is looking at a map. The activity shown is backpacking in a natural environment. The girl in the photo may have chosen this activity because she likes to be alone and free.

I would enjoy doing this activity. I love being free in the outdoors, wandering through the countryside, discovering new places. When I'm on my own, I can give all my attention to the place I'm visiting.

I would not enjoy doing this activity. Going backpacking alone in the countryside would bore me. I prefer to do things with my friends. And when we go on holiday, we want fun and action.

MAIN COURSE

Unit 5 The virtual world

1 WORKING WITH WORDS

1	Regardless	5	engage	9	exceeds
2	adult	6	isolated	10	avoid
3	several	7	poll		
4	appear	8	average		

2 LOOKING AT THE TEXT

1 The average British person spends one hour on social media per day.
2 Women check their pages more often than men.
3 More than 3.6 million Britons use Twitter for more than two hours a day.
4 Facebook was voted the most popular social media site by 59% of people polled.
5 People avoid being isolated by spending several hours online every day.
6 Rebecca Dye is the social media manager at *first direct* online bank.
7 Rebecca Dye means that people don't write letters or emails and don't phone each other or meet up in person as much these days.
8 Rebecca Dye's company will interact more with its customers on social media.

3 BUILDING SKILLS

A

c

B

1 isolation, frustration, loneliness, felt need to use Facebook app
2 focus on the household (housework), spend more time with family (daughter)

4 GETTING IT RIGHT

1	went	6	thought	11	looked	16	rang
2	opened	7	was	12	Were	17	was
3	checked	8	found	13	did	18	left
4	found	9	didn't	14	didn't	19	understood
5	was	10	sat	15	couldn't	20	had to

5 LISTENING

A

1 False. Margaret Green phones Catherine Seale.
2 True
3 False. She thinks they're in London.
4 False. She's in her car.
5 False. She told him not to have any parties.
6 True
7 False. A boy is trying to break in.
8 False. Gatecrashers are blocking the street.
9 True
10 False. The riot police stopped the people wrecking the front garden.

B

1	vomiting	3	trash	5	revellers
2	skylight	4	gatecrashers	6	flight

C

(Lösungsvorschlag)

Margaret Green drove her son Jamie to the party at Christopher Seale's house. When she arrived, she saw hundreds of young people in the street and in the front garden. The music coming out of the house was extremely loud. Jamie got out of the car, walked up to the house, rang the doorbell and waited. Nobody opened the door, so he pushed it open and went inside.

When the door opened, Mrs Green saw young people dancing wildly and shouting. Suddenly, she heard a crash. It came from the roof. She looked up and saw a teenager standing on the roof. The next thing Mrs Green saw was the riot police. They jumped out of their vans and started to break up the crowd outside the house. Mrs Green then realised that things were out of control, so she phoned Catherine Seale. She thought the Seales were out for the evening. She didn't know that they were on holiday in France.

6 GETTING IT RIGHT

1	hasn't used	6	spent
2	used	7	hasn't been
3	1 has changed; 2 made	8	has changed
4	1 weren't; 2 felt	9	1 has started; 2 has done
5	1 told; 2 were	10	1 told; 2 played

BUSINESS OPTIONS

1 Most people have stressful lives and prefer to spend their free time on the couch rather than in a store.
2 People who shop online often use search engines to find the store they want.
3 Virtual stores collect information about you like your age, social group and how much money you have.
4 Shoppers often feel frustrated browsing through the aisles of physical stores only to find the item they want is not in stock.
5 Traditional stationary stores have a hard time competing with online stores.

Unit 6 Advertising

1 LOOKING AT THE TEXT

A

1	e	3	i	5	a	7	d	9	h
2	g	4	c	6	j	8	f	10	b

B

1 False. Few people recycle their glass.
2 False. It gives you points.
3 True
4 False. It is much more successful.
5 True
6 False. It's on the ground.
7 True
8 False. In one day people threw in 72kg of rubbish.

2 BUILDING SKILLS

Correct order: d, f, i, h, b, j, c, l, k, g, e, a

3 LISTENING

A/B

A Definition	B Description
Product	top brand perfume and cosmetics
Promotion	special reductions of up to 40%
Price	£40 for 50 ml of top brand perfume; £12 for a 75 ml top brand deodorant stick
Place	in-flight only

4 GETTING IT RIGHT

A

1 I'm sure wearables will be a great success in the near future.
2 We are launching the whole range in Edinburgh on Monday.
3 Each member of my team is going to demonstrate a different sort of wearable.
4 I'm going to wear a waterproof Android watch.
5 We're having a press conference at 9 am.
6 We believe that demand for wearables will double in the next six months.

B

1. we're/I'm going to introduce
2. they'll make
3. We're/I'm going to start
4. you'll be
5. you'll see
6. is competing
7. She's taking
8. she'll win
9. we're/I'm going to ask
10. will win

5 BUILDING SKILLS

A

1. 7 May 1946
2. 10 (13 incl. MiniDisc, MP3 player and Android Walkman)
3. PlayStation network was hacked (77 million accounts compromised)

B

1. Famous inventions
2. World market
3. Mobile entertainment
4. Major setbacks

C

(Stichworte)

1. brought out transistor radio, changed name to Sony
2. to access the world's largest consumer market
3. light and portable transistor radio and Walkman enabled people to listen to radio and music anywhere, not just in one place
4. laptops and PCs

6 BUILDING SKILLS

1	gives	5	shows
2	has increased	6	has risen
3	rose	7	is
4	went	8	haven't stopped

BUSINESS OPTIONS

1	E	2	D	3	A	4	B	5	C

Unit 7 Family and beyond

1 WORKING WITH WORDS

A

1	borrow	5	noisy
2	long-distance	6	forget
3	extended	7	together
4	criticize	8	huge

B

1. **1** local; **2** long-distance
2. **1** noisy; **2** quiet
3. **1** remember; **2** forgot
4. **1** together; **2** separately
5. **1** extended; **2** nuclear
6. **1** huge; **2** tiny
7. **1** borrow; **2** lend
8. **1** criticize; **2** praise

2 GETTING IT RIGHT

A

1. who came to England first
2. which was very poor
3. which paid very little
4. which would offer a better future
5. who was hiring workers for a UK textile company
6. who were offered jobs
7. which followed their arrival
8. who never gave up on anything

B

1. which made us decide to
2. she knew she might soon lose
3. which was doing badly
4. the company had already got rid of
5. who had to go next
6. the EU financial crisis hit very badly
7. who pushed for us to move here
8. I've been most worried about

3 WRITING AN INFORMAL LETTER

53 West Road
Dublin 22
Ireland

29th May, 20…

Dear Grandma and Grandpa

This is to say a big 'thank you' for the money you kindly sent me for my birthday. I'm going to put it towards some beautiful shoes I really, really want! I'll be able to show you them when we get home for Christmas next month. I can't wait for that because I miss you all and the family so much. So do Mum, Dad and Sam.

Well, I must stop now and run to catch the post. Thank you again!

Lots of love
Lisa

4 WORKING WITH WORDS

A

1	in	2	in/at	3	in	4	at

B

1	at	6	in front of	11	above
2	near	7	behind	12	across
3	opposite	8	beyond	13	below
4	next to	9	around	14	In/On
5	Between	10	on		

5 GETTING IT RIGHT

1	were living / lived	9	was looking for
2	weren't getting on / didn't get on	10	were
		11	was trying / tried
3	was cleaning up / cleaned up	12	opened
		13	had to
4	had	14	was looking forward
5	kept	15	looked
6	were all cooking	16	was
7	had	17	shouted / were shouting
8	started	18	agreed

6 BUILDING SKILLS

1	Keighley	5	7 Bow Road, Wendcot
2	Carole Elisabeth	6	AL7 8NB
3	17	7	07765188399
4	13th October		

BUSINESS OPTIONS

(Lösungsvorschläge)

1 It has unfortunately become normal in society for people to expect men to be decisive and make decisions quickly. The stereotype for women is that they don't know much about cars and so would need longer to decide on a product.

2 I think that both men and women can be knowledgeable about a specific subject, but people have expected men to somehow know more about cars since the beginning of the twentieth century.

3 This graphic does not describe me because I am female but know a lot about cars and would be confident to buy one.

4 I would model the adverts for men and women based on how they prefer to purchase cars. For example, for men I would emphasize the brand of the car and for women its features.

Unit 8 Entering the world of work

1 LISTENING

1 16
2 –
3 community service group
4 art, English, sport: basketball and football
5 chemistry, biology
6 baby-sitting
7 work placement in a kindergarten, an old people's home or a hospital
8 17
9 top DJ, DJ headliner at the Ultra Music Festival in Miami
10 DJ incl. *Your Mum's House* night club
11 sport, (body-building)
12 all other subjects, especially history
13 Saturday job in a jeans shop; worked in a tattoo studio
14 learn a musical instrument or study music, stay on at school and take exams

2 LOOKING AT THE TEXT

A
1 one month minimum
2 €1,000 + tips + overtime
3 cottage in hotel complex
4 free
5 (keine Angabe)
6 max. €300 for return airfare from home country

B

1	application	4	tip	7	located
2	leisure	5	waiter/waitress	8	range
3	experience	6	willing		

3 BUILDING SKILLS
(freie Lösung)

4 WORKING WITH WORDS

1	gradual	4	downsize	7	filing cabinet
2	workforce	5	property	8	Human Resources
3	challenge	6	requires		

5 GETTING IT RIGHT

A

1	won't have	6	'll/will put
2	don't apply	7	change
3	send	8	'll/will be
4	'll/will tell	9	won't find
5	contact	10	wait

B

1	'd/would be	6	saw
2	had	7	'd/would accept
3	worked	8	meant
4	'd/would deal	9	Would you take
5	'd/would be	10	came

6 BUILDING SKILLS

A

1	There are several questions to think about when discussing	5	Another point to consider is this:
2	In my opinion	6	On the one hand
3	firstly	7	on the other hand
4	secondly	8	As a consequence
		9	On the whole
		10	To conclude

B
(freie Lösung)

BUSINESS OPTIONS

1	females	4	quotas	7	conclusion
2	founders	5	aim	8	male
3	ratio	6	equal		

Unit 9 Multiculturalism

1 BUILDING SKILLS

C
(Lösungsvorschläge)

1 He grew up in an Afro-Caribbean community / among Jamaicans / in an area he calls 'the Jamaican capital of Europe'.
2 He could not read or write when he left school at the age of 13.
3 The BBC poll showed that he was one of the country's most-loved poets / He was voted the UK's third most-loved poet.
4 This might surprise us because he attacks many things that are part of British culture.
5 He refused the (offer of the) OBE because he is against anything that has a connection with the British Empire.

2 WORKING WITH WORDS

A
1 performance
2 poetry, poem
3 politics
4 song

B
1 singer
2 songs
3 politicians
4 politics
5 performer
6 performances
7 poet
8 poems

3 GETTING IT RIGHT

1 If unemployment had not been so high in Britain, Tom would have found work without much difficulty.
2 If he had got a job in the UK, he would have stayed in Britain quite happily.
3 If things had gone well for him, he would not have wondered about work in other countries.
4 If he had never been to Australia, he is certain he would never have thought about working somewhere so far away.
5 If he had not looked for work there though, he would have missed the perfect job for him – as a tour guide for visitors.
6 If he had not taken a tour group up the Gold Coast, he would never have met the perfect girl for him, and champion surfer Jenny would never have become the love of his life!

4 GETTING IT RIGHT

1 had gone
2 gave
3 had expected
4 had never visited
5 began
6 was
7 had experienced
8 received
9 had happened
10 learned
11 had disappeared
12 read
13 had been
14 explained
15 had finally found

5 LISTENING

1 14.1   2 31.1   3 5   4 8   5 13

6 BUILDING SKILLS

A
1 rose
2 under
3 almost exactly
4 reached
5 little change
6 increase
7 rapidly
8 around
9 approximately
10 downwards
11 fall
12 less than

B
1 fall
2 upwards
3 rose / increased
4 rapidly
5 over / more than
6 approximately / almost exactly

C
(Lösungsvorschlag)
Since 2012, the figures have risen again to levels that the country last saw over a century ago. The latest statistics show that the immigrant population has continued to rise and has reached (00.0) million, approximately (00)% of the present US population of (00.0) million.

BUSINESS OPTIONS

1 slang words
2 shake hands
3 intercultural competence
4 eye contact
5 personal space
6 set up
7 advertising campaign
8 market share

Unit 10 Helping others

1 WORKING WITH WORDS

1 producer
2 charity
3 to donate
4 donor
5 complaint
6 sponsorship
7 accountancy
8 to empower
9 amazing
10 safe
11 companionship
12 homeless

2 BUILDING SKILLS

A
1 the Netherlands (or the UK)
2 the USA
3 Turkey and France
4 the UK
5 Germany

B
1 percentage
2 clearly
3 place
4 ranks
5 column
6 value
7 twice
8 half

C
(Lösungsvorschlag)

Whereas private American individuals donate the most money to help others, their government donates the least money. The UK government is the biggest giver donating 0.72% of GNI and UK individuals are the second biggest givers with individual giving at 0.73% of GDP. While French individuals donate the least money, the French government gives twice as much as the US government with 0.41% of GNI compared to 0.19%. The Turkish government gives almost twice as much (0.42%)

than private individuals in Turkey (0.23%) whereas the Australian government actually gives almost half as much (0.34%) as Australian individuals do (0.69%).

3 LOOKING AT THE TEXTS

A
1 True
2 False. They were 200 km away (from the British Embassy).
3 Not in the text
4 False. They were strong because they were taught to think of the needs of others first.
5 Not in the text
6 False. They were inspired by Gandhi, who always wore flip-flops.
7 False. It's a registered charity.
8 True

B
1	siblings	4	strength	7	survival
2	advice	5	humanitarian	8	charity
3	hitchhiked	6	orphanages		

4 LISTENING

1	b	3	c	5	b	7	a
2	a	4	a	6	b	8	c

5 GETTING IT RIGHT

A
1 I've [have] asked
2 Have I asked?
3 I haven't asked
4 You've [have] driven
5 Have you driven?
6 You haven't driven
7 She's [has] fallen
8 Has she fallen?
9 She hasn't fallen
10 We've [have] felt
11 Have we felt?
12 We haven't felt
13 They've [have] worn
14 Have they worn?
15 They haven't worn

B
1 I've [have] been asking
2 Have I been asking?
3 I haven't been asking
4 You've [have] been driving
5 Have you been driving?
6 You haven't been driving
7 She's [has] been falling
8 Has she been falling?
9 She hasn't been falling
10 We've [have] been feeling
11 Have we been feeling?
12 We haven't been feeling
13 They've [have] been wearing
14 Have they been wearing?
15 They haven't been wearing

C
1 have written
2 have sold
3 have been selling
4 has been wearing
5 has bought
6 has donated
7 has started
8 has been working
9 's/has been serving
10 have bought

1 B   2 A   3 C

Unit 11 Global reach

1 WORKING WITH WORDS

A
1	an order	3	contact	5	action
2	a contract	4	quality		

B
1	made a mistake	6	filled the position
2	fills a need	7	make a complaint
3	take place	8	take advice
4	lost heart	9	lose sight of
5	raise a question	10	raise our prices

2 GETTING IT RIGHT

A
1 Coffee is grown organically by farmers from all over the Gumutindo district.
2 Then the coffee is brought to the new central production facility.
3 There, quality and quantity are checked by highly-trained senior staff.
4 Then the raw coffee is processed in carefully-controlled conditions.
5 After that, the coffee is packed by the Cooperative's new, automated equipment.
6 Finally, the finished product is sent to Mombasa for export to Europe and America.

B
The ACE FURNITURE factory here in Virginia has been closed by the company owners in New York, and 200 workers have been thrown out of their jobs. The decision was made last summer, but the workforce was not told till last month. All the equipment from the Virginia plant will be sent to a new factory in Indonesia, and the same furniture will be produced there for a quarter of the pay.

But when production is moved offshore like this, American jobs are exported, too, and the American economy is damaged. If every US factory is closed, the US economy will be completely destroyed. Then who will all those 'made in Asia' products be bought by?

3 BUILDING SKILLS
(Lösungsvorschlag)

The cartoon shows a manager and one of his workers in the manager's office. He is sitting at his desk, and he is telling his employee that he is going to fire him. He is explaining that the employee has been replaced by someone in China who is better at his job and who is also cheaper to employ.

This is an ironic comment on globalization's effects on ordinary working people's lives in the West. It reminds us that the developed economies are no longer competitive with economies in the Far East, and that many US and European jobs have been exported to the developing world. Because of this, Western workers are faced with an uncertain future in the world of work.

The manager is sitting comfortably, and he is talking to the other man apparently without any sympathy. The cartoonist is attacking the way that business destroys people's lives without any human feeling. As far as the manager is concerned, the employee is just a piece of equipment that he is replacing with a better piece of equipment.

4 LISTENING

A
1. 500 (no change)
2. 500 – 0
3. 0 – 1,000
4. 1,000 – 1,500
5. 1,500 – 1,600
6. 1,600 – 1,400
7. 1,400 – 800

B
8. remained unchanged
9. rapid fall
10. climbed rapidly
11. steady increase
12. slight further increase
13. declined steadily
14. sharp further decrease

5 BUILDING SKILLS

A
(freie Lösung)

B
In the first half of Year 3, sales increased slowly from zero to 500 kilos (per month). Then in the second half there was a steady further rise to 1,500 kilos (per month). In the first half of Year 4, sales climbed only slightly to a (monthly) total of 1,700 kilos. But since then there has been a rapid growth in sales from 1,700 to 3,000 kilos (per month).

BUSINESS OPTIONS

1. Buddhist
2. shelter
3. housing
4. burden
5. literacy
6. starvation
7. anonymous
8. improve
9. Christian

Unit 12 Changing society

1 WORKING WITH WORDS

A
daytime TV, entry-level job, job application, middle management, minimum wage, pay packet, production assistant, retail industry, university degree, welfare system

B
1. minimum wage
2. retail industry
3. production assistant
4. middle management
5. welfare system
6. entry-level job
7. university degree
8. job applications
9. daytime TV
10. pay packet

2 GETTING IT RIGHT

A
1. needn't
2. should
3. can
4. don't have to
5. must
6. shouldn't
7. can't
8. have to
9. may
10. might

B
1. 1 haven't been able to; 2 can
2. 1 could; 2 couldn't
3. 1 can't; 2 was able to
4. 1 couldn't; 2 was able to

3 LISTENING

A
Name: Peter North, age: 83, years at WPRH: 2
Wife: Lucy (died 12 years ago)
Children: 3 – 2 sons & 1 daughter
Grandchildren: 6 – ages from 18 to 2
Interests: art class, music (mostly jazz), day trips

B
1 T, 2 F, 3 F, 4 F, 5 T, 6 F, 7 T

C
2. He lived on his own for ten years, before moving to Windsor Park two years ago.
3. He moved to Windsor Park because it was getting hard to look after everything.
4. His two sons and his daughter all have families.
6. They took him out to a restaurant.

4 GETTING IT RIGHT

Rules for visitors
1. Whenever possible, visits should be planned for normal visiting hours. (However, visits may be allowed at other times by special arrangement.)
2. Please note that sometimes a visit may not be allowed if a resident is very unwell.
3. Visitors must be signed in at reception.
4. We are sorry, but pets cannot be brought into the building.
5. You are welcome to eat with us, and visitors' meals can be ordered by phone or email 24 hours in advance.
6. All communication with staff is very welcome, but nurses should not be interrupted when preparing residents' medications.

5 BUILDING SKILLS

a 2
b 6
c 1
d 5
e 3
f 4

BUSINESS OPTIONS

1. True
2. False: She is a university student.
3. False: He believes that feedback is important and interns should know what they are doing well and what they could improve.
4. False: Ms Monk believes internships should be paid, but Mr Patel believes that sometimes the experience is more important than the payment. Companies are more willing to give interns a chance if they don't have to pay.
5. True
6. False: Ms Monk thinks that the interns shouldn't receive exactly the same pay and conditions as other employees because then the educational value gets lost.

7 False: Ms Monk's campaign wants businesses to have to give interns a minimum amount of pay, training and legal rights.

8 False: Ms Monk thinks if you are an intern at a company where you don't feel like you're learning enough, you should talk to somebody in charge.

9 True

10 True

EXAM PREPARATION

Unit 13 The challenges of the modern state

1 LOOKING AT THE TEXT

A

b

B

(Lösungsvorschläge)

1 Young girls are leaving the UK to become jihadi brides in the Middle East. They run away from home and seldom come back.

2 They have launched a campaign called 'Making A Stand' to stop young girls from running away. (The campaign includes a letter describing the conditions the girls will live under in an ISIS caliphate.)

3 According to the ISIS leader, a young Western woman can expect a new life and a chance to contribute to the creation of a pure Islamic state. Women can expect a variety of jobs and responsibilities, such as joining the all-female moral police force to make sure women keep to the specific ISIS interpretation of Sharia law.
According to *Making A Stand*, a young woman can expect to be married from the age of 9 and to be kept veiled and out of sight. She can expect to be treated as a second-class citizen, and to lose her individuality and dignity. She will be unable to either fulfil her dreams in the caliphate or return to the West.

4 A young woman might have been born in the UK and have enough money, but still feel socially isolated. She might suffer from depression and feel like she doesn't belong in the West because of restrictions on how Muslims can practise their religion. A young woman might decide to run away and become a jihadi bride because of personal and political reasons, but also because of naive romanticism.

2 WRITING

(freie Lösung)

3 WORKING WITH WORDS

A		**B**	
1	terrorist	1	fulfil
2	remind	2	terrorists
3	succeed	3	freedom
4	fulfil	4	restrictions
5	freedom	5	practise
6	treat	6	dignity
7	dignity	7	reminds
8	promise	8	succeed
9	migrant	9	treat
10	violence	10	violence
11	restriction		
12	practise		

4 LISTENING

1 b   2 c   3 b   4 c   5 a   6 a

5 GETTING IT RIGHT

1	to open	7	using
2	to download	8	changing
3	to shop	9	to be
4	giving	10	to have / having
5	doing	11	to lose
6	to provide	12	having

6 BUILDING SKILLS

1 If you ask me

2 The main reason is

3 What's your view on

4 I couldn't agree more

5 Well, as a matter of fact

6 I'm afraid I can't accept

7 I see what you mean (or: There's some truth in what you say)

8 there's some truth in what you say (or: I see what you mean)

9 Let me put it in another way

10 do you see what I mean

11 So is the basic idea that

12 I'm sorry to interrupt, but

BUSINESS OPTIONS

1	overwhelming exhaustion	4	healthy eating
2	repetitive work	5	summer hours
3	dysfunctional attitude	6	study leave

Unit 14 Energy and the environment

1 WORKING WITH WORDS

1	lift	4	stop	7	opportunity
2	hugely	5	appear		
3	reason for	6	grew		

GETTING IT RIGHT

A

(Lösungsvorschlag)

Sally Miller stated that climate change was nothing new because it was happening all the time: it always had (done), and it always would. So she didn't think that the Greens could blame humans for something that was just part of nature.

Mark Farina did not agree. He pointed out that there was a clear connection between the rise in CO_2 levels that had begun with the Industrial Revolution and the warming that the world had seen since then. He went on to say that the more CO_2 people threw into the atmosphere, the more temperatures would continue to rise.

B

1 Kate asked if/whether her newspaper often sent her on jobs like that.
2 Chris wanted to know how long she had been away.
3 Lisa wondered if/whether she had interviewed anyone interesting.
4 Ellie inquired what she had talked to Matt Radley about.
5 Tom asked if/whether he had answered her questions properly.
6 Jean inquired if/whether she had written her report yet.
7 Tom wanted to know when they could read it in the paper.
8 Ben wondered where she thought they would send her next.

C

The Brussels trip had been Julie's first big job, so her editor Tony Good wanted a meeting about it. He called Julie and told her to come to his office for a chat as soon as she was free. Julie asked him to give her a bit longer so that she could finish her report. So Tony gave her a time, and he also requested her to email him the report before she came to let him have a quick look at it. Julie agreed, and then she asked him to (perhaps) suggest ways she could improve it.

Before the meeting, Tony contacted the Features Editor, Tania Ray, and invited her to come to his office to discuss Julie Branson's report. Both the editors liked the report, but Tony advised Julie to reduce it by about 100 words so that they could include a visual. Then he called Alan Carter in the Art Department and instructed him to prepare a visual that would show the fracking process. Finally, at the end of the meeting, Julie made a big request. She begged Tony to send her to find out how local people felt about the fracking project.

3 LISTENING

1	d	3	b	5	c
2	a	4	f	6	e

4 WRITING

A

a 3b & 6e; **b** 2a & 5c; **c** 1d & 4f

B

(Lösungsvorschlag)

What do local people think about the fracking project? I found that opinions were very varied, and here are just a few of them.

Stella King, an office worker who is expecting her first child, thought that it was essential to reject the fracking project because of the constant noise from heavy vehicles and the danger of accidents. However, Bob Lowe, a jobless engineering worker and father of three, felt that it was fine to accept some temporary problems as everything would be quiet and peaceful for many years after that.

Lyn Benson, a nursery teacher and mother of two, believed that although it would cause temporary problems, it would bring investments that would produce permanent future benefits. However, Alan Smith, aged 20 and an apprentice mechanic, complained that the project would make a few rich people even richer, but that it would bring nothing but trouble to the whole community.

Jenny Wade, a student and a Greenpeace supporter, argued that it was wrong to develop new fossil fuel sources, but that it was essential to rely just on renewable energy sources to protect the future of the Earth. However, Brian Fox, aged 78, a retired builder and four-time grandfather, accepted that renewables could not produce enough power yet, so it was very important to have power till then from a cleaner source than coal or oil.

BUSINESS OPTIONS

1	remove	7	share
2	mend	8	spend
3	run out	9	forward
4	earn	10	scale down
5	increase	11	lend
6	add	12	benefit

Unit 15 Feeding the world

1 WORKING WITH WORDS

A

1	greenhouse gases	4	global warming
2	climate change	5	natural resources
3	environmental pollution	6	carbon emissions

B

1	natural resources	4	greenhouse gases
2	environmental pollution	5	global warming
3	carbon emissions	6	climate change

C

1	agriculture	9	consumption
2	exploitation	10	groundwater
3	farmland	11	drought
4	forests	12	cooperation
5	ecosystems	13	infrastructure
6	crops	14	irrigation
7	species	15	famine
8	diet		

GETTING IT RIGHT

While growing up in London, Joe Dean loved going to help his aunt and uncle on their farm in the country in the school holidays. Then before going to college at the age of 18, he spent the summer as a volunteer on an organic farm. While studying economics for the next three years, he took summer gardening jobs to make money. Before getting a 'proper' job at the end of college, he volunteered for six months at CEFS. Then after joining a big financial organization in London, he specialized in investing in environmentally-friendly agriculture. After continuing with this work for several years, he started dreaming of leaving and running his own project. Then while visiting his aunt and uncle, now in their sixties, he began talking about his ideas, and they invited him to run their farm for them. Since taking over his aunt and uncle's farm, he has introduced organic farming and a lot of new techniques.

3 **WORKING WITH WORDS**

A
1–4 disease, drought, pests, weeds
5 + 6 crops, livestock
7 + 8 fertilizer, herbicide
9 + 10 pollution, runoff
11 selective breeding
12–15 GM technology, hydroponics, organic practices, vertical farms

B
1 weather
2 fertilizer
3 herbicide
4 problems
5–8 disease, drought, pests, weeds
9 +10 crops, livestock
11 unwanted waste products
12 + 13 pollution, runoff
14 agricultural improvements
15 selective breeding
16–19 GM technology, hydroponics, organic practices, vertical farming

4 **GETTING IT RIGHT**

For over 200 years, there have been people saying that famine would soon kill millions and predicting a great reduction in the human population. For example, enormous famines predicted in the 1960s for India and other parts of the world did not happen. Certainly, the scenes of African starvation often shown on our TV screens have been real and terrible enough. However, the fact is that scenarios warning of hundreds of millions of deaths have not come true – at least, not yet.

This is largely thanks to a green revolution created just in time by new varieties of rice, wheat and other crops. These varieties developed by selective breeding in the 1960s produce far more food per acre with much greater reliability than before.

However, the productivity push given to farming by this revolution is coming to an end, even while the population goes on rising rapidly. The race continuing

ever more urgently today is to create a new green revolution to get us through the next half century.

5 **LISTENING**

A
2 burgers: £4.80
2 portions of French fries: £3.20
2 colas: £1.80
Fast-food price total: £9.80

2 portions of chicken: £3.10
½ kilo of potatoes: £0.60
Vegetables: £3.80
Fruit: £1.20
1 litre of milk: £0.90
Supermarket price total: £9.60

B
a Some people love this sort of food.
b Other people don't like cooking.
c Others don't know how to cook.
d Fast food takes less time and trouble.

C
A *Fast food*
a Going there & back: 15
b Ordering: 5
c Eating: 15   Total: 35

B *Home-cooked*
a Shopping: 45
b Preparing: 45
c Eating: 20
d Washing up & tidying up: 15   Total: 125

BUSINESS OPTIONS

1	vast	7	drought
2	frequent	8	livestock
3	prison	9	constitution
4	civilian	10	forced labour
5	election	11	displace
6	settle	12	poverty

Unit 16 Technology

1 **WORKING WITH WORDS**

1	access	8	click
2	mobile	9	message
3	programmer	10	laptop
4	email	11	provider
5	function	12	network
6	online	13	Internet
7	credit	14	communication

2 **WORKING WITH WORDS**

A
1	remind	3	rebuild	5	redevelop
2	reproduce	4	rethink	6	rewrite

B
independent, illegal, impossible, informal, illiterate, irregular

C

1 **1** impossible; **2** possible
2 **1** literate; **2** illiterate
3 **1** independent; **2** dependent
4 **1** irregular; **2** regular
5 **1** legal; **2** illegal
6 **1** formal; **2** informal

3 GETTING IT RIGHT

1 is waiting / I'll (I will) lend
2 had to go / he was able to
3 has Carl been doing / He's been
4 a few / two pairs of trousers
5 was signed / must be paid
6 had already gone / I was waiting
7 told me / now she is/she is now
8 Did you go / I'm going to spend/I'm spending

4 LISTENING

A/B

1 (A&E) hospital nurse; opinion d
2 road construction company director; opinion a
3 car insurance salesperson; opinion f
4 city planning officer; opinion c

5 WRITING

A

(Lösungsvorschlag)

I agree with Sylvia Ray, the A&E hospital nurse. I think driverless cars are an excellent new technology, and she is right to be for them. I really believe that they will greatly reduce the number of road accidents and save precious medical resources, which can then be used to deal with other needs.

I disagree with Ben Miller, the road construction company director. I do not think driverless cars are a terrible new technology, and I feel he is wrong to be against them. I really do not think it matters a lot that they will reduce demand for his company's services and cause unemployment in his industry.

B

(Lösungsvorschlag)

The in-car entertainment designer is for driverless cars, but the car repair workshop owner is against them. On the one hand, the designer is excited that they will offer new opportunities to develop communication and other technologies that will help drivers use their free time. On the other hand, the workshop owner is worried that it will not be possible to repair expensive hi-tech vehicles when they break down, and that this will destroy many small businesses like his.

BUSINESS OPTIONS

1 When do the bathrooms on the map turn green?
   When they are not occupied
2 Who created the live map?
   Houghton and his colleagues
3 What is the design of the app supposed to encourage?
   Ad hoc social interactions and make it easy to find people
4 Why was Houghton kicked out of the ladies' room?
   It was the women's private space and they didn't want any spaceship-looking sensors.
5 What is sinister about the app?
   Being able to watch a colleague's every move
6 Does Houghton have plans to sell the software?
   No, it's just for internal use

Topic 1 Personalized advertising

1 WORKING WITH WORDS

1	personalization	8	special offers
2	suit	9	advert
3	purchase	10	related
4	bargain	11	creepy
5	recommended	12	invasion
6	retailers	13	consumer experience
7	ability	14	uncomfortable

2 SENTENCE STRUCTURE

(Lösungsvorschläge)

1 Do you see adverts when shopping?
A I often see adverts when shopping.
2 Are the adverts helpful?
A I like the adverts' suggestions.
3 Do you find the adverts creepy?
A I think it's creepy that companies gather information about me when I shop online.
4 Do you sometimes get emails with special offers?
A I often get emails with special offers.

3 WORKING WITH WORDS

1	inappropriate	7	manager
2	seem	8	identification
3	presume	9	appointment
4	book	10	wear
5	occasionally	11	regular
6	voucher	12	apply

Topic 2 Built-in obsolescence

1 WORKING WITH WORDS

A

1	d	3	a	5	h	7	e
2	f	4	c	6	g	8	b

B

1	repair shop	5	smartphone upgrade
2	private details	6	in operation
3	survey sheet	7	Consumer attitudes
4	note down	8	even though

2 WORKING WITH WORDS

1	cheap	5	previous
2	fragile	6	durable
3	stylish	7	costly
4	slim		

3 DESCRIBING A CARTOON

(Lösungsvorschlag)

The cartoonist is suggesting that businesses purposefully programme problems into their hardware so that consumers have to upgrade their products after a while instead of trying to fix them. It has become normal to simply buy a new product because we are so used to things breaking. The cartoonist doesn't agree with this because only the businessmen who own the company benefit from it and he/she shows this by showing that the businessmen in the picture are smiling and are very satisfied with their plan.

4 ODD ONE OUT

1	big	3	keep	5	weak
2	after	4	fix		

Topic 3 Saturation from advertising

1 WORKING WITH WORDS

A

1	ambush sb	7	escape
2	backfire	8	permission
3	grab sb's attention	9	project
4	paint	10	memorable
5	warfare	11	inexpensive
6	junk mail	12	buzz

B

1	warfare	7	junk mail
2	ambushed	8	buzz
3	paint	9	inexpensive
4	projected	10	escape
5	permission	11	backfires
6	memorable	12	grabs your attention

2 WORKING WITH WORDS

1	surroundings	5	neglected
2	racist	6	collective
3	reflect	7	1 amused; 2 amusing
4	lucky	8	raise awareness

3 WORKING WITH WORDS

(Lösungsvorschläge)

1 What a cute **puppy**.
2 You have to buy a ticket at the **ticket machine**.
3 The child is looking at his **reflection**.
4 The man is **surrounded** by women.
5 No one is on the **platform**.

Topic 4 Styles of business leadership

1 WORD FAMILIES

A

NOUN	VERB	ADJECTIVE
collaboration	collaborate	collaborative
boredom	bore	boring
priority	prioritize	prioritized
exclusion	exclude	excluded
bully	bully	bullied
adoption	adopt	adopted
sound	sound	sounding
filter	filter	filtered

B

1 sounded
2 filtered
3 bored
4 prioritize
5 collaborative
6 bully
7 exclusion
8 adoption

2 WORKING WITH WORDS

1 power structure
2 run smoothly
3 self-motivated
4 trouble-maker
5 be vocal
6 try out
7 iron out
8 in contrast
9 one size fits all
10 like-minded
11 make happen
12 fit in

Topic 5 Global workplaces and mergers

1 SENTENCE STRUCTURE

1 By merging the two companies, the owners thought that they would be more profitable.
2 Although there were branches in London and New York, the headquarters were in Paris.
3 The boss had to rearrange the offices because two of the colleagues sharing an office were incompatible.
4 Once a year, I have a meeting with my boss in which she assesses my performance.
5 All of the new employees at our company receive a handbook when they start which gives them information about who works for the company and what the standard procedures are.
6 I felt insecure when I first started the job, but the longer I worked there, the more I understood my tasks and after a few weeks, I felt much better.
7 Putting in more effort to make sure the project was finished on time definitely paid off.

2 WORKING WITH WORDS

1 expertise
2 economical
3 imposes
4 scrap
5 pays off
6 dress code
7 insignificant
8 stabilizing
9 unhappy
10 unsolved

3 LOOKING AT THE TEXT

A

1 … cooperating with their new colleagues from Germany.
2 … standoffish and unfriendly.
3 … the collegial atmosphere in the company would suffer.
4 … they worked less efficiently than was expected.
5 … they were late to meetings and then tried to initiate small talk.
6 … were easily offended.

B

(freie Lösung)

Topic 6 Corporate social responsibility

1 WORKING WITH WORDS

A

1	A	6	L	11	G
2	E	7	O	12	F
3	I	8	C	13	M
4	B	9	D	14	J
5	N	10	K	15	H

B

1 Social responsibility
2 corporate governance
3 clear conscience
4 human rights
5 developing world
6 factory floor
7 fair trade
8 end customer
9 labour practices
10 locally sourced

2 WORKING WITH WORDS

1 shareholders
2 contentment
3 entire
4 nutritious
5 stock
6 junk food
7 discourage
8 approval

3 MUDDLED SENTENCES

4	A	12	F	1	K
8	B	7	G	3	L
13	C	6	H	2	M
9	D	11	I		
5	E	10	J		

Topic 7 Population, wealth and refugees

1 WORKING WITH WORDS

1	charity
2	overpopulation
3 (across)	famine
3 (down)	flee
4	unlikely
5	capitalism
6	twice
7	dull
8	shelter
9	innovator
10	persecution
11	refugee

2 LOOKING AT THE TEXT

A
1 F
2 T
3 F
4 N
5 T

B
1 … they are worried about the cost of re-homing them and what it will do to the economy.
2 … working as entrepreneurs, innovators, being taxpayers, consumers and investors.
3 … the country's economic opportunities and world output are boosted.
4 … dull or difficult jobs that locals spurn, like cleaning offices and caring for the elderly.
5 … they have more younger workers receiving wages and paying taxes.
6 … stop seeing refugees as a burden to be shared but rather as an opportunity to be welcomed.

3 WRITING A COMMENT

(Lösungsvorschlag)

Many people are concerned about the refugee situation but Legrain seems to think it can help economic growth rather than hurt it. I think he might be right. The asylum seekers could take jobs that other people already living in the country aren't interested in and they will be contributing taxpayers to the economy.

Topic 8 The future job market

1 WORD FAMILIES

A

1	memory	11	personalize
2	advertise	12	personalization
3	demand	13	communicative
4	demand	14	communication
5	advance	15	orbiting
6	advancement	16	orbit
7	prolonged	17	amaze
8	prolongation	18	amazing/amazed
9	customized	19	painful
10	customization		

B

1	advertisement	5	memorize
2	customize/personalize	6	communicate
3	personalized/ customized	7	amazed
4	painful	8	demanding

2 WORKING WITH WORDS

A

1 j	3 b	5 l	7 d	9 h	11 c
2 e	4 a/i	6 f	8 k	10 i/a	12 g

B

1	open up	7	tour guide
2	job opening	8	set guidelines
3	entry-level	9	body part
4	physical work	10	storage capacity
5	medical science	11	manual labour
6	body language	12	silent observer

3 ODD ONE OUT

1 job opening – the other three are people in the interview process
2 physical work – the other three are jobs
3 customized – the other three are part of your body
4 pianist – the other three are science/medical related fields

Topic 9 Technological advances and cybercrime

1 WORKING WITH WORDS

A

(siehe Seite 18)

B

1	witness	10	ruthless
2	drone	11	framework
3	furious	12	transportation
4	determine	13	societal
5	craziness	14	capture
6	mock	15	alter
7	competition	16	incompetent
8	insult	17	mankind
9	breathtaking	18	violate

C

1	alter	5	framework
2	witnessing	6	societal
3	drones	7	competition, ruthless
4	determined	8	capture

Topic 10 Crops, chemicals and genetic mutation

1 WORKING WITH WORDS

A

1	controversy	8	labelling
2	long-term	9	known
3	widespread	10	regulators
4	discouraging	11	complications
5	vulnerable	12	outcry
6	farmers	13	provoking
7	pesticides		

B

Text 1 – supports, Text 2 - opposes

2 COMMENTING ON A CARTOON

(Lösungsvorschläge)

A

1 The cartoon is referring to milk.
2 The cartoon is talking about genetically modifying milk so that different varieties of milk (for example soy milk) can be milked straight from the cow.
3 It is funny that a cow would be able to produce different types of milk depending on our needs.

B

The cartoon shows a cow who has been genetically modified so that it can produce different types of milk, for example soy milk or skimmed milk. By giving the cartoon the title 'The miracle of genetic engineering' the cartoonist is making the point in a funny way that genetic engineering could make our lives easier. Lifestyle choices nowadays, for example being vegan, or allergies to milk mean that there is a big market for different

types of milk and it would be great if all of these different kinds could come straight from the cow.

3 WORKING WITH WORDS

1 environmentalists
2 presidential nomination; block
3 opposition; monopoly; seed; off the market
4 banned; elementary

Topic 11 Sustainable agriculture

1 WORKING WITH WORDS

A

1	l	5	m	9	e	13	j	17	g
2	n	6	a	10	i	14	f		
3	o	7	c	11	h	15	d		
4	k	8	p	12	b	16	q		

B

1	social housing	7	rooftops
2	awareness	8	funds
3	coop	9	rise
4	backyard	10	well off
5	supply	11	diminishes
6	bees		

2 LOOKING AT THE TEXT

(Lösungsvorschläge)

2 Animal agriculture destroying rainforests
3 Just eat vegetarian meals one day a week
4 Animal farms and greenhouse gases
5 Animal waste causes pollution
6 Use food to feed the hungry not animals

Topic 12 Industrial Revolution 4.0

1 WORKING WITH WORDS

A

(siehe Seite 19)

B

1	radical	6	trackers
2	evolved	7	rest/sleep
3	pockets	8	sleep/rest
4	implementing	9	optimization
5	paperless	10	establishing

2 BRAINSTORMING

(freie Lösung)

TOPIC 9, EXERCISE 2, WORD SQUARE (WB, P. 80)

VERBS	ADJECTIVES	NOUNS
1 determine	1 breathtaking	1 competition
2 violate	2 incompetent	2 mankind
3 insult	3 furious	3 craziness
4 mock	4 ruthless	4 drone
5 capture	5 societal	5 framework
6 alter		6 transportation
7 witness		

N	O	I	T	I	T	E	P	M	O	C	D	W	N	Q	V	V	I
Q	B	R	E	A	T	H	T	A	K	I	N	G	I	M	D	M	C
Y	W	Z	O	Z	Q	F	U	D	E	T	E	R	M	I	N	E	C
E	S	U	O	I	R	U	F	F	R	V	R	S	K	F	A	I	F
T	R	L	D	E	Z	H	Q	J	A	Q	T	A	F	K	O	D	N
J	R	X	Z	T	T	S	X	J	R	J	K	Y	Q	N	E	E	Z
M	J	A	Y	L	I	A	T	V	C	U	W	W	T	F	N	W	L
A	E	W	N	U	A	K	L	N	L	R	T	L	U	O	O	A	A
N	R	I	J	S	Q	I	V	O	E	G	E	H	R	T	W	P	T
K	U	T	V	N	P	R	D	W	I	T	V	D	L	L	O	F	E
I	T	N	A	I	L	O	A	K	M	V	E	K	C	E	R	E	I
N	P	E	P	L	R	L	R	C	C	H	U	P	M	A	S	K	C
D	A	S	M	N	T	T	K	T	K	O	B	I	M	X	T	S	O
R	C	S	B	E	R	D	O	N	A	N	M	E	X	O	N	E	S
O	R	K	R	T	Y	T	G	V	C	T	W	Q	T	V	C	J	I
S	S	E	N	I	Z	A	R	C	F	O	I	R	H	L	J	N	N
C	D	G	H	B	Q	J	Z	U	R	L	X	O	K	V	N	F	I
V	P	P	E	P	C	R	H	K	Q	R	J	Y	N	I	P	R	N

TOPIC 12, EXERCISE 1, WORD SQUARE (WB, P. 86)

1 biometric
2 energetic
3 enjoy
4 establish
5 even

6 evolve
7 implement
8 lock
9 mattress
10 optimization

11 paperless
12 pattern
13 pocket
14 radical
15 rest

16 seamlessly
17 set
18 sleep
19 swipe
20 tracker

D	C	K	I	Z	G	H	L	M	J	I	W	P	K	T	U	N
S	H	X	L	P	P	O	N	J	C	C	G	I	T	H	S	V
L	M	G	K	M	I	M	P	L	E	M	E	N	T	O	M	P
X	K	W	I	U	H	S	I	L	B	A	T	S	E	J	P	R
E	P	R	R	T	E	K	C	O	P	N	R	E	T	T	A	P
Y	X	A	L	N	N	Z	T	K	E	F	J	K	W	B	V	G
L	E	N	E	R	G	E	T	I	C	Q	H	C	Z	I	S	L
S	T	O	P	T	I	M	I	Z	A	T	I	O	N	O	Y	N
S	P	W	T	G	I	S	J	I	Y	S	T	L	N	M	H	F
E	S	A	K	S	L	L	A	C	I	D	A	R	H	E	L	S
L	X	W	P	X	E	V	O	L	V	E	B	J	E	T	V	R
M	T	B	I	E	O	R	N	W	R	E	K	C	A	R	T	E
A	V	E	Y	P	R	E	R	R	S	E	G	X	D	I	P	J
E	S	D	Z	A	E	L	N	G	N	K	H	E	M	C	P	H
S	D	R	W	Q	P	A	E	J	M	S	K	T	U	F	U	O
M	A	T	T	R	E	S	S	S	O	O	P	E	E	L	S	E
A	L	Z	N	W	R	H	Y	W	S	Y	Q	C	V	S	E	T

19

Audioscripts

Unit 1, Exercise 7B

Desirée   Hi Patrick.

Patrick   Hi Desirée. I am calling from my car. What are you doing at the moment?

Desirée   I'm reading the latest report about us in the newspaper.

Patrick   What story is the press making up now?

Desirée   That you're dating another woman.

Patrick   These people are going too far. Are they trying to split us up?

Desirée   I suppose they are only doing their job. Oh, no! Two reporters are walking up the path to the front door.

Patrick   Don't worry, darling. I'm driving into your street right now. I can see them. Hey, you!

Unit 2, Exercise 6

1

Interviewer   Good morning, Jane. Thanks for agreeing to talk to our listeners about keeping fit. You do aerobics, I believe?

Jane   That's right. As far as I'm concerned, aerobics is one of the best ways to stay healthy. It strengthens the heart and the lungs and it's also a great way to reduce stress. It's exactly the right thing for me after a long day at work.

Interviewer   Yes. I can imagine that all those powerful moves help to get rid of stress. How often do you do aerobics?

Jane   I go to a class once a week, but I also do aerobics at home. I just put on some music and do the moves.

Interviewer   What would you say to anyone thinking about doing aerobics as a way to keep fit?

Jane   It's a fun way to keep fit and it's not too expensive. You don't really need any special clothes and once you've paid for the class, all you have to do is get there on time, join in and have fun.

Interviewer   So what you're saying is that doing aerobics offers quite a few health benefits. It's good for the heart and the lungs and the muscles. And it helps you get rid of stress. It's fun and it's not expensive so, if you're thinking of doing something to keep fit, why not do as Jane does, join an aerobics class and have fun!

2

Interviewer   I've come to the local swimming pool where I'm talking to Will about swimming as a way to keep fit. Good evening, Will. Thanks for your time.

Will   No problem.

Interviewer   To begin with, why have you chosen swimming as a way to keep fit?

Will   Well, you exercise every bit of your body and it's a great work-out. It's also a very relaxing activity, so it helps me to sleep well. The main reason why I go swimming, though, is to get slim and stay slim. I gave up sport when I left college and then I started to get fat. I've lost two kilos since I started swimming regularly.

Interviewer   That sounds great, Will. It's a good work-out and helps you sleep and you're losing weight, too.

Will   That's right. I'd definitely recommend swimming as a good way to keep fit. You don't have to have a great body to go swimming. People of all shapes and sizes go swimming.

Interviewer   Thanks, Will. Just to go over what you said: when you swim, you exercise every part of your body. Swimming helps you relax, so you can sleep well and it also helps you lose weight. So, all you listeners, if you feel you need any of these benefits, it doesn't matter what you look like, get your swimming gear on and jump in!

3

Interviewer   The last person I'm talking to today is Lily. She's just finished an exciting game of volleyball. Hi, Lily. How was the game?

Lily   My team didn't win, but everyone had a lot of fun. That's one of the good things about volleyball. Even if you lose a game, you still feel great afterwards.

Interviewer   Anything that gives you a good feeling must be good for your health. What about the other health benefits of playing volleyball?

Lily   Well, it certainly burns calories. That's not why I took up volleyball, though. I've never been overweight. No, when I started college, I wanted to get to know people so I looked for a team sport. The people in the volleyball team here at college were really nice, so I joined the club.

Interviewer   Team sports certainly are a good way to get to know people.

Lily   Definitely, every team sport helps you make friends. You're working together to get the best result and that makes you feel good, too.

Interviewer   And that's another health benefit, eh? Well, listeners, what about volleyball as a way to keep fit? It's a lot of fun, it makes you feel great and it burns up calories. It's a team sport and, as Lily said, team sports help you make friends, and working together with them for a good result keeps you healthy, too. Thanks, Lily.

Unit 3, Exercise 4

Oh, dear. I'm not sure which of these three phones to choose. I can see that the Universe is bigger than the NeatPhone and the Bright is the biggest of all three, but I'll have to think some more.

How heavy are they? The NeatPhone is lighter than the two other phones. The Universe is not as heavy as the Bright. The Bright is heavier than the other two.

What does it say here about the battery life? The battery life of the NeatPhone is not as long as the battery life of the Bright. It looks as if the batteries of the Universe last longest.

What about the price? Well, the Bright is the cheapest of the phones. The NeatPhone is more expensive than the Bright and the Universe is the most expensive of them all.

Oh, I don't know which of these three phones is best. Choosing a phone is one of the most difficult things to do in life. Hmmm. I think I'll buy the NeatPhone. It's the lightest and it looks the nicest. Yes. It's the NeatPhone. That's the one I'll buy.

Unit 5, Exercise 5

Catherine	Hello?
Margaret	Oh, hello. Am I speaking to Catherine Seale?
Catherine	Yes, that's right. Who's speaking, please?
Margaret	It's Margaret Green. Your son Christopher and my son Jamie are in the same class at school.
Catherine	Ah, yes I remember! I think Jamie was at our house a few weeks ago. If you're trying to reach Christopher, please try him on his mobile because my husband and I are on holiday in France at the moment.
Margaret	In France! Oh dear! I thought you were here in London. Well, I think I understand better what's happening now because I've just brought Jamie to your house for the party and …
Catherine	Party! What party? I told him not to have any parties!
Margaret	Well, there's certainly one going on in your house at the moment. I'm in my car outside and I think it's out of control. There are young people everywhere, some are drunk and vomiting in the front garden and I think I can see someone on the roof.
Catherine	On the roof! That can't be true! Oh my god, what's happening?

Margaret	I think the boy on the roof is trying to open the skylight. I think he's trying to break in. It doesn't look good here, Catherine. There's very loud music and from what I can see they're all dancing wildly in the front room.
Catherine	On my new carpet! They'll trash it! Can't you stop them somehow?
Margaret	I'm not sure but can you hear that siren?
Catherine	Siren? You mean the police siren?
Margaret	Yes, the riot police are here now and they're breaking up all the people blocking the street and in the front garden.
Catherine	The riot police are breaking up the people blocking the street! How many are there outside the house?
Margaret	I would say hundreds. I'm so sorry to tell you all this but I think they must be gatecrashers because Jamie said Christopher only invited 60 people and was going to have a bouncer to make sure nobody else got in.
Catherine	I just don't believe this! Is my son Christopher there?
Margaret	I can't see him. He must be inside but I don't want to go in there with all those drunken revellers. Anyway, the riot police have stopped the people wrecking the front garden now.
Catherine	My husband has been listening and we're getting the first flight back to London! Thanks for letting me know, Margaret.
Margaret	Don't mention it and have a nice flight!

Unit 6, Exercise 3B

We hope you're enjoying your flight with High Sky Air Travel. In a few moments, you will have the chance to take advantage of our super in-flight perfume and cosmetics prices, which are up to 40% cheaper than on the high street. Yes, you heard it right! As a passenger on a High Sky flight you have the chance to buy top brand perfume and cosmetics up to 40% cheaper! These prices are valid until just before we land in London, so this is a real chance for you to save money. For example, why not buy a 50 ml bottle of a top brand perfume for just £40 and save £15 pounds on high street prices? Or a 75 ml top brand deodorant stick for men for just £12 compared to £20 in your local store? These are just two examples of our unbelievable offers. Pay by card or cash in pounds or euros when our cabin crew come by and ask them to show you what other great deals we have for you.

Unit 7, Exercise 6

Officer	Well, Carrie, let's start with some personal details, shall we?

Carrie	Fine, yes.
Officer	So first, can I have your family name?
Carrie	It's Keighley.
Officer	Could you spell that for me, please?
Carrie	Yes. It's K-e-i-g-h-l-e-y.
Officer	Right, and your first name? What is Carrie short for?
Carrie	Carole – with an 'e' on the end. And my middle name is Elisabeth. That's spelt with an 's', not a 'z', by the way.
Officer	So your given names are Carole – C-a-r-o-l-e – Elisabeth – E-l-i-s-a-b-e-t-h.
Carrie	That's right.
Officer	And what age are you now?
Carrie	I'm 17 now. My birthday was last month. The 13th of October.
Officer	The 30th of October?
Carrie	No, the 13th.
Officer	Thanks, so that gives me your date of birth … And now can I make a note of your home address, please?
Carrie	Yes, it's 7 Bow Road, Wendcot.
Officer	OK, so that's 7 Bow Road, Wendcot. And the post code?
Carrie	It's AL7 8NB.
Officer	AL7 8NB. Good, and now your phone number?
Carrie	I'll give you my mobile, all right?
Officer	That's fine.
Carrie	It's oh-double-seven-six-five …
Officer	Oh-double-seven-six-five …
Carrie	One-double-eight-three-double-nine.
Officer	Double-one-eight-three-double-nine.
Carrie	No, sorry. That's one-double-eight-three-double-nine.
Officer	Oh, right. Good. Now, let's talk about your situation at home …

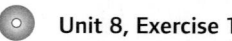

Unit 8, Exercise 1

Dialogue 1

Advisor	Good morning, Meera.
Meera	Good morning.
Advisor	Please take a seat.
Meera	Thanks.
Advisor	I'm very glad you've come, Meera, because it's a good idea to start planning your career early, and 16 is a good age to start. The first thing I'm going to do is ask you a few questions to find out what sort of person you are. Alright?

Meera	Yes, fine.
Advisor	What's your dream job?
Meera	Dream job … er … I'm not sure, really. I don't really know.
Advisor	Don't worry. Not many people can answer that question. What activities do you do outside school in your free time?
Meera	Well, I signed up for our school's community service group and we visit people who need some help. For example, there are mothers with young children who need help at home, sometimes just holding the baby or playing with the toddlers. And then there's an old man near the school who needs a bit of shopping done. That kind of thing.
Advisor	That's very helpful information, Meera. Now what about your subjects at school? Which ones do you like most?
Meera	Well, I love art! I won the art prize last year for a painting I did and it's still up on the wall in the entrance to our school as you come in. And I like English, of course. I like to read stories about what life is like for young people in other countries. That sort of thing. Oh, and I forgot sport. I like basketball and football, too.
Advisor	And are there any subjects you don't like?
Meera	Chemistry! I really don't know why we do it. Biology is hard work, too.
Advisor	Well, I'm getting a picture of you now, Meera. Do you have any work experience?
Meera	No, not really.
Advisor	Not helping out in a shop, giving out leaflets, baby-sitting or anything like that?
Meera	Oh, yes baby-sitting, of course! That's not work. That's fun!
Advisor	And do you get paid for it?
Meera	Oh, yes. I'm always being asked by friends and family. Last month I made almost a hundred pounds!
Advisor	Well, I think I have a picture of you now, Meera. I think you might like a job looking after people, young or old, so I think you should do a work placement in a kindergarten, an old people's home or a hospital and then come back to me.
Meera	A kindergarten would be nice.
Advisor	Here's a list of addresses to contact … *(fade)*

Dialogue 2

Advisor	Good morning, Christopher.
Christopher	Hi.
Advisor	Please take a seat.
Christopher	Thanks.

Advisor	I'm glad you've come to see me, Christopher, because I think 17 is a good time to think about planning your future.
Christopher	Look, to be honest I'm here because everybody in my year has to see a careers advisor when they're 17. I already know what I want to do and on my 18th birthday I'm going to walk out of school and do it.
Advisor	Before your exams in May?
Christopher	Yes. My 18th birthday's in March, so I can leave on the day I'm 18.
Advisor	That's a big decision to make, Christopher. You're doing well at school. I can see that from your good results. Do you really dislike school that much?
Christopher	It's meaningless. I see my friends there but I'm basically just wasting my time.
Advisor	So you already know what your dream job is?
Christopher	Yes, I'm going to be a top DJ and my ambition is to be a DJ headliner at the Ultra Music Festival in Miami. I don't need school for that, do I?
Advisor	I see. How much do you know about the job?
Christopher	Well, in my free time I'm a DJ. And in the holidays I had a guest DJ residency at Your Mum's House. It was great!
Advisor	And Your Mum's House is the name of a nightclub?
Christopher	Yes, it's a number one club. I've played there and they want me back.
Advisor	Well, I can see you know a lot about music and that you are very ambitious, but I still have some questions I'd like to ask you. Is that alright?
Christopher	Fire away.
Advisor	What are your favourite subjects at school?
Christopher	None.
Advisor	Is there absolutely nothing you like at school?
Christopher	The only thing I like doing there is sport because I want to keep fit. A DJ has to look good and I like to work out. Once we did some body-building in sport and that was good.
Advisor	OK, sport and body-building and you don't like anything else at school?
Christopher	No, nothing, and of all the things I don't like, history's the subject I hate most of all.
Advisor	Alright, and apart from DJ'ing do you have any other work experience?
Christopher	I had a Saturday job in a shop selling jeans. It was alright but nothing special. And I worked in a tattoo studio. That was good and I got some cool tattoos.
Advisor	Well, I think I have a good picture of you now, Christopher.
Christopher	Good. Can I go now?
Advisor	Yes, of course, I don't want to keep you here against your will, but have you ever thought about learning a musical instrument or studying music? As you spend all your free time working with music, it would help you in your career – but you'd need to stay on at school and take your exams to study music.
Christopher	Hm, I suppose studying music could be helpful. I'll think about it …

Unit 9, Exercise 5

9

Presenter	Welcome to *Behind the News*. Well, US immigration is a hot political topic again, so let's take a look at it. To help us, Professor David Newman is going to talk us through the facts and figures. Well now, Professor Newman, America is a country of immigrants, isn't it? So are today's immigration numbers really so dramatic?
Newman	Well, yes and no. Way back, over a century ago, the statistics were quite similar to the figures today, so the situation now isn't new. But in between, something different happened. You see, from the early 1900s, there was a long, long fall in immigration that continued till around 1970. By that time, immigrant numbers were low – around 9.6 million out of a population of just over 200 million. That meant that the immigrant share of the population was only about 5%.
Presenter	So what's happened since then?
Newman	Well, since then, the figures have risen quite rapidly. By 1980, the number of immigrants was around 6% of the population. That was a total of 14.1 million people. And the trend continued. By 1990, the immigrant population had reached 19.8 million out of a total of just under 250 million. As a percentage, that was about 8% of the total. Then by the start of this century, in the year 2000, we see another big jump to 11% of the total population. By that time, there were 31.1 million immigrants in America.
Presenter	And more recently?
Newman	Well, in 2012, the total population was approximately 313.7 million. At the same time, the immigrant population reached 40.8 million. That was around 13% of

the whole US population. This took US immigration back to the levels that used to arrive in America around a century ago. And the trend is still rising today.

Unit 10, Exercise 4

In this podcast we'll hear how a charity set up by a survivor of the 2004 Boxing Day tsunami has provided emergency relief to people whose lives were destroyed.

Clare Allen and her daughter Daisy were on holiday in Sri Lanka when the tsunami struck. Luckily, the huge waves stopped just short of her hotel and her daughter, who had been on the beach, was found safe. The tsunami killed 40,000 people in Sri Lanka and left over a million homeless, so emergency help was desperately needed. After her miraculous escape, Clare decided to set up a charity, which she called *Rebuilding Sri Lanka*, and since then the charity has built 300 homes, a special needs school, two schools for young children, five libraries and an English language centre, to name just a few of its achievements.

One of its many projects is called 'Books and Buns', meaning education and food for children of school age. In many parts of Sri Lanka the school buildings have not been improved or repaired for decades and children who wish to pass their school-leaving exams have to pay for extra lessons and spend about £2,000 on school books. This makes it impossible for poor children to get a good education, so *Rebuilding Sri Lanka* has built modern libraries with new and up-to-date school books. Its largest library has over 2,700 members and every Saturday more than 200 books are borrowed from it.

Poor children often walk long distances to school and arrive tired and hungry, so *Rebuilding Sri Lanka* gives meals to over 5,000 schoolchildren a day. The result is a 23% increase in school attendance.

Its other projects include finding jobs for the unemployed, supporting hospitals with medical supplies and equipment and a Children's Resource Centre where traumatized children, some of whom have lost one or both parents, can receive counselling.

Rebuilding Sri Lanka is proud of the fact that its website designers, accountants and fundraisers all work for free, meaning that only 5% of the money it collects is spent on administration. 95% of donations are therefore used to help people in need.

Unit 11, Exercise 4

So now we can look back over the four years since the Gumutindo Coffee Cooperative was formed, and we can see that things have gone really well – after a slow start.

In the first half of Year 1, sales rose gradually from zero to around 500 kilos a month. They then remained unchanged at that level for the rest of Year 1. In Year 2, the change to organic production took place, and this meant a rapid fall to zero again for a short time at the end of the first half. However, organic sales then took off well in the second half, and they climbed rapidly to 1,000 kilos a month by the end of the year. In Year 3, there was a steady increase in sales to 1,500 kilos a

month by the end of the first half. This was at the same time as processed coffee production began – the now-famous Gumutindo Gold Brand. This soon affected sales of unprocessed coffee, and so there was only a slight further increase to 1,600 kilos by the end of Year 3. And this year, Gold Brand sales have really taken off. Because of this, sales of unprocessed beans declined steadily to 1,400 kilos a month in the first half, and since then, in the second half, there has been a sharp further decrease to just 800 kilos per month.

Now, Gold Brand has been a huge success story, as we all know, so let's now take a look at sales of this product.

Unit 12, Exercise 3

Carlos	Hello? Can you see me?
Peter	Yes, I can see you just fine. Hello there. And who am I speaking to?
Carlos	My name's Carlos Branco.
Peter	Well, hi. And I'm Peter North. Nice to meet you.
Carlos	And it's good to meet you too, Mr North. Thank you for agreeing to talk to me like this on Skype.
Peter	Oh, please just call me Peter. Anyway, I'm only too happy to try this Skype idea. It's nice to see a new face – especially a young one! Now how do you want to do this?
Carlos	Maybe we should tell each other a little about ourselves. Er … would you like to start?
Peter	Sure. Well, I'm Peter North, as I said, and I turned 83 years old yesterday.
Carlos	Wow! Happy birthday! And have you been at Windsor Park for long?
Peter	For about two years. Until then, I lived alone for many years, but it was getting hard to look after everything.
Carlos	Do you have any family?
Peter	Well, sadly my wife Lucy died twelve years ago.
Carlos	I'm sorry to hear that.
Peter	But I have three children – two sons and a daughter.
Carlos	And do you have any grandchildren?
Peter	Yes, six! All my children have children of their own.
Carlos	Fantastic! And what sort of ages are they?
Peter	They go all the way down from 18 to just two.
Carlos	They must be fun!
Peter	They are. And you know what? All three families came yesterday to take me out for a birthday party at a really nice restaurant. It was a big surprise. I couldn't believe my eyes when they all came through the door!

24

Carlos Wow! A very special day! But tell me, what do you usually do from day to day at Windsor Park? Do you have any special interests?

Peter Oh, yes, there are lots of things you can do here. For example, I go to an art class every Wednesday. I listen to a lot of music, too – mostly jazz. And when they organize day trips for the residents, I always try to join them. It's nice here, but you have to get out when you can.

Unit 13, Exercise 4

Host Good evening and welcome to our live radio show *Across the country*. Our topic this evening is surveillance cameras. We've all noticed them and some of us feel safer when we see them but others certainly don't. It's estimated that there are almost six million CCTV cameras across the UK and new cameras are being installed every day, so do we just need to accept them or is now the time to do something before it's too late? Our studio guests are Detective Inspector John Langton, journalist Sally Herald, Student's Union representative Megan O'Hara and actor Johnny Pitt. We'll also be reading out your emails, texts and tweets to hear your views. Let's start off the discussion with Detective Inspector Langton. How do the police see surveillance cameras?

Inspector The British public have the right to feel safe wherever they are, day and night, seven days a week, 52 weeks a year and we, as the nation's police force, have to make sure this happens. That's why we use everything possible to do our job. That includes surveillance cameras. Whether it's the student whose mobile is stolen, the old lady who has her handbag taken or the terrorist who leaves a bomb in a public place – we need to act fast and surveillance cameras often give us the information we need. I believe they help to make the UK a safer place.

Host Sally Herald, as a journalist, do you share the police's opinion?

Herald Well, I wouldn't be a journalist if I did! There's some truth in what he says, of course, but that's not the whole story. We, in the UK, have become camera-mad! We have cameras in places we don't expect them and certainly don't need them! The whole country's camera-crazy but I think we just don't notice them anymore.

Host And what are these places where we don't expect or need them?

Herald Schools and hospitals, for example. These places are full of people with eyes in their heads! Why do we need cameras?

Host Well, we've heard two very opposing views now, so Johnny Pitt, you spend a lot of time in front of cameras. Do you also like them to watch you in the street when you're going about your daily business?

Pitt Well, I guess I find it normal to see cameras everywhere. The world is a dangerous place and I think that if people know there's a good chance that there's a camera recording them, they'll think twice before breaking the law. Privacy is of course important but I'm willing to lose some of it to stay safe if it reduces crime.

Host Megan O'Hara, you represent the UK's student community. What do you think about the importance of personal safety and privacy?

O'Hara I want safety *and* privacy. I don't agree that it's a question of one or the other. There was personal safety before we had cameras everywhere and now we have more and more cameras and less and less personal safety. As for privacy, we can forget it! Not only do we have surveillance cameras recording our every move, whistleblowers now tell us that hackers can secretly turn on our mobile phone cameras, so how do we know the police aren't doing this, as well? I also don't agree with Johnny Pitt that cameras will make people think twice before breaking the law. Cameras may help the police *after* a crime but they don't *stop* crimes.

Host Would you like to comment on that Detective Inspector Langton?

Inspector The police don't break the law, Ms O'Hara! We defend it and we use all legal methods to protect citizens of this country, no more and no less.

O'Hara Oh really! It didn't look like that at our last student demonstration when the police …

Host Let's stick to the point, please. Sally Herald, do you agree that cameras can prevent crimes?

Herald Well, I certainly don't agree with Johnny Pitt on that point. We all remember that picture of him punching a photographer outside his hotel, so I don't think he thinks twice before breaking the law!

Pitt That was self-defence! The guy was in my way and wouldn't move. It just looked like a punch!

Herald That's not what the doctor said at the hospital! I interviewed him personally and he said he thought the photographer had been hit by a boxer. I'm sure you were making a boxing movie at the time …

Host	I think it's time to hear our listeners' comments. We have a tweet from …

Unit 14, Exercise 3

Jenny Wade	I think it's crazy to take any more fossil fuels out of the ground when we know that climate change is getting out of control. Now, what we need to do is to invest everything in renewable forms of energy. That way, we'll have a chance of saving the world for our children and grandchildren.
Stella King	I'm really worried about the noise, with big trucks going along our narrow roads at all hours, day and night. And think how dangerous it will be for us all – especially for our children. We mustn't allow this development to take place.
Lyn Benson	It probably won't be easy for the community for a while, that's for sure. But they're promising to put a lot of money into the community in return, and that will do some real good for all of us far into the future.
Brian Fox	I'm old enough to remember times when the lights went out, and it wasn't nice. We've already closed down a lot of the old coal-fired power stations, and it'll be years before renewables can replace them. And gas is a lot cleaner than coal, so we should use that to keep the lights on for the next 20 years.
Alan Smith	Why should we support this fracking project? It doesn't make any sense, does it? I mean, this is the sort of thing that'll give a lot more money to people who already have a lot of money. And what do we local people get in return? Nothing – nothing but trouble!
Bob Lowe	I think we should welcome this development even if it means accepting some noise and a bit of a hard time for a few months. Remember: after those few months, production will continue year after year without any more problems. That seems all right to me – especially as I may be able to get a job!

Unit 15, Exercise 5A

So you're hungry, but let's say you've only got £10 to spend. What will you buy – fast food or fresh food to cook for yourselves?

Well, if you go to your local fast-food restaurant, it's all very simple. You'll be able to get two burgers that cost £2.40 each for a total of £4.80. With those, of course, you'll want two portions of French fries and they'll cost you another £3.20. After that, well, you need something to drink and two medium colas will cost £1.80. Is there enough for any extras – fruit yogurts, perhaps? Well,

no, because you've already spent £9.80 on your rather basic dinner for two.

Now, if you go to the supermarket, you'll get more for your money. For two portions of chicken, you'll need to pay £3.10. Half a kilo of potatoes will be yours for just 60 pence. Then allow £3.80 for some healthy salad vegetables. You can get some fruit, too, for another £1.20. And finally, you can get a litre of milk for just 90 pence. Total: £9.60 and you've got yourselves a good, healthy dinner for two that won't leave you hungry in the middle of the night!

Unit 15, Exercise 5B

So why does anyone choose fast food? Well, they might prefer to eat fast food for various reasons. First of all, some people just love this sort of food. After all, these big fast-food chains do a lot of research on creating food that's tasty – food that people want to come back for again and again. Secondly, there are also lots of people who really don't like cooking very much. It's too much of a chore, and they're more interested in their work or in other things. Thirdly, these days there are other people who really don't know how to cook. They just never learned, perhaps because their own parents were too busy to teach them. And finally, of course, fast food is what it says it is: fast. In today's busy world, a lot of people have to rush round all the time – perhaps between two different jobs, for example. For them, fast food just takes less time and trouble than a home-cooked meal.

Unit 15, Exercise 5C

So just how much time and trouble do these different types of meal take? Well, let's think about your local fast-food restaurant first. Let's say going there and back takes 15 minutes. Then when you're there, you have to order what you want and then wait for a short time, so let's say ordering takes five minutes. And after that, there's just the eating, and it isn't a very big meal, is it? So let's say eating takes another 15 minutes. That's a total of 35 minutes and you're all done.

But now what about the home-cooked meal? Well first you've got to go and get everything from the shop and then get home again. So let's say shopping takes 45 minutes. Then there's preparing the food – washing the vegetables, cooking and so on. So let's allow another 45 minutes for preparing. Now comes the good bit – eating! Well, you've got quite a big meal, so that should take another 20 minutes. Then, finally, there's washing up and tidying up to do after that. Not so nice, but very important. And let's allow 15 minutes for that. That's a total of 125 minutes all together. Over two hours in other words!

Unit 16, Exercise 4

Mark Moro	Now let's open the debate about driverless cars to our studio audience. First, please, the lady in the green jacket.
Sylvia Ray	Thank you. I'm Sylvia Ray and I'm an A & E nurse. Every day I see the horrible results of road accidents – accidents

usually caused by human error. So I'm in favour of this new technology. It seems to me that driverless cars have the potential to cut the number of deaths and injuries on the roads. We don't have as many emergency service staff and doctors and nurses as we need, and you know what? Thanks to driverless cars, we'll now be released to handle more of the other medical problems we're trained to deal with.

Mark Moro   Thank you. All right, well now let's hear from the man in the grey suit.

Ben Miller   I'm Ben Miller. I'm the Director of Right Road Construction and, as you might expect, I think driverless cars are a terrible idea! If they can really drive very close together, that means we'll never need to build any more roads. That'll cut the need for the work my organization does – road construction. The only thing anyone will want us for is to repair the roads and bridges we've already got. Thinking about the whole road construction industry, that'll cost lots of jobs. I don't want to see that.

Mark Moro   Thank you. So we've now had one view in favour and one view very much against driverless cars. Now the young lady in the yellow blouse.

Julie North   Thank you. Well, I'm Julie North and I'm a car insurance salesperson, and from a personal point of view I'm against driverless cars. If they really and truly mean a much higher level of safety, then that will bring down the amount drivers have to pay for their car insurance. And that can only mean one thing: many of the people selling car insurance like me will have to start again – maybe training to sell other sorts of insurance instead.

Mark Moro   Thank you. Well, I can see that would be a problem for some people, though a lot more people would be very happy to see the cost of driving come down like that. All right, let's have one more opinion now. The man in the blue jacket, please.

Peter Hill   I'm Peter Hill. I'm a city planning officer, and I have to say that I'm very much in favour of this new technology. I want our cities to work more efficiently, and one of the really inefficient things is the way traffic moves – or doesn't move. A lot of the time, cars are parked on roads or in great big car parks. Now driverless cars will be shared by lots of people, and so that problem will mostly disappear because these cars won't need to be parked for long. As soon as one person has driven into the city centre, for example, the car can be called to someone else. It'll drive straight there, pick up the next person and drive to the next place.

a My computer isn't working properly: things keep disappearing from the screen. _____

b Cut the pastry into circles and then work them into little cups to hold the mixture. _____

c I'm only working part-time at the moment, so I'm looking for a full-time job. _____

d I worked it so that Tom and Ann sat together at dinner and had a chance to talk. _____

e It'll take three people for us to be able to work this old machine properly. _____

f The medicine started to work almost immediately, and Sam soon began to feel better. _____

BUSINESS OPTIONS

Look at the interview on page 118 of the student's book and decide whether the following statements are true or false. Correct the false statements.

→ Rezeption: Leseverstehen, SB S. 214

1 Sahil Patel is the head of a successful software company.

_____

2 Catherine Monk is the CEO of a company which offers internships to university students.

_____

3 Mr Patel does not believe that feedback is necessary when a person is doing an internship.

_____

4 Ms Monk and Mr Patel think that it is very important that internships are paid.

_____

5 Mr Patel thinks that the value of networking and learning during an internship can be more important than how much money one earns.

_____

6 Ms Monk thinks that interns should receive the same amount of payment as regular employees.

_____

7 Mr Patel's company wants businesses to have to give interns a minimum amount of pay, training and legal rights.

_____

8 Ms Monk thinks that if you are an intern at a company where you don't feel like you're learning enough, you should quit.

_____

9 Mr Patel thinks it is important to keep in contact with the people you interned for after you leave the company.

_____

10 Mr Patel and Ms Monk agree that internships are a valuable experience for university students.

_____

1 LOOKING AT THE TEXT

→ Grobverständnis, SB S. 214

A Skim the text quickly and decide which statement best describes what it is about.

a Young Muslim girls from poor families are running away to the Middle East.

b Young Muslim girls who run away feel that Western society doesn't value them.

c Recent migrants are more in favour of terrorism.

UK MUSLIM COMMUNITY
DEVASTATED BY RUNAWAY JIHADI BRIDES

The press regularly write stories about young European men leaving to become foreign fighters in the Middle East and returning to Europe as hardened terrorists, but it took a little longer for society to realize that young girls were also leaving and rarely coming back. The UK's Muslim community is so *devastated* that in September 2014, Muslim women launched the 'Making A Stand' campaign to stop their children, in particular their daughters, running away and joining extremist groups in the Middle East.

In a moving letter to all young Muslim girls thinking of going out to join ISIS, they remind them that in the ISIS *caliphate*, girls should marry from the age of nine and women wear *veils* and are kept out of sight of society. They tell them that once in Syria or Iraq they will not be allowed to leave the caliphate and return to the UK, adding that many have tried but few have succeeded. They warn the young Muslim girls that they will have no chance to fulfil any dreams they may have about a better life and will lose their identity and freedom, because ISIS treats women as second-class citizens and not with the *dignity* and respect they are promised in Islam.

So what makes a young person decide to run away? A University of London study found that young Muslims *sympathizing* with terrorism were often born and brought up in the UK, had enough money but were socially isolated and suffered from depression. Recent migrants to the UK who came to the West to escape violence and war were found to be less ready to support radical ideas.

Another study found that Western society does not give young Muslims the feeling that they belong. Instead, they feel that society does not value them and in some cases places *restrictions* on how they can *practise* Islam, e.g. the burka ban in France and Belgium. It describes how the leader of ISIS offers young women a new life in which they can help create a pure Islamic state with a variety of jobs and responsibilities for women, such as being a member of an all-women moral police force which makes sure that other women *keep* strictly *to* ISIS's interpretation of Sharia law. The study finishes by saying that the young women's reasons for joining the jihadis in the Middle East are not only political but also personal, with a strong element of naive romanticism. (408 words)

Vocabulary notes					
devastated	*am Boden zerstört*	dignity	*Würde*	to practise	*ausüben*
caliphate	*Kalifat*	to sympathize	*sympathisieren*	to keep to	*einhalten*
veil	*Schleier*	restriction	*Einschränkung*		

B Answer the questions about the text in exercise 1 in your own words as far as possible.

→ Umgang mit Operatoren, SB S. 232

1 Outline the problem that has shocked the UK's Muslim community.

2 Describe the action taken by the Muslim community to counteract this problem.

3 Contrast the life that a young Western woman can expect in the ISIS caliphate as described by its leader and by the members of *Making A Stand*.

4 Examine the factors which may make a young woman decide to become a jihadi bride.

2 WRITING

→ Eine Stellungnahme schreiben, SB S. 234

Write a comment on the topic of jihadi brides. Evaluate the explanations given in the text and comment on the roles played by the young women's friends, family, religious community and school.

3 WORKING WITH WORDS

A Complete the word families using forms from the text in exercise 1.

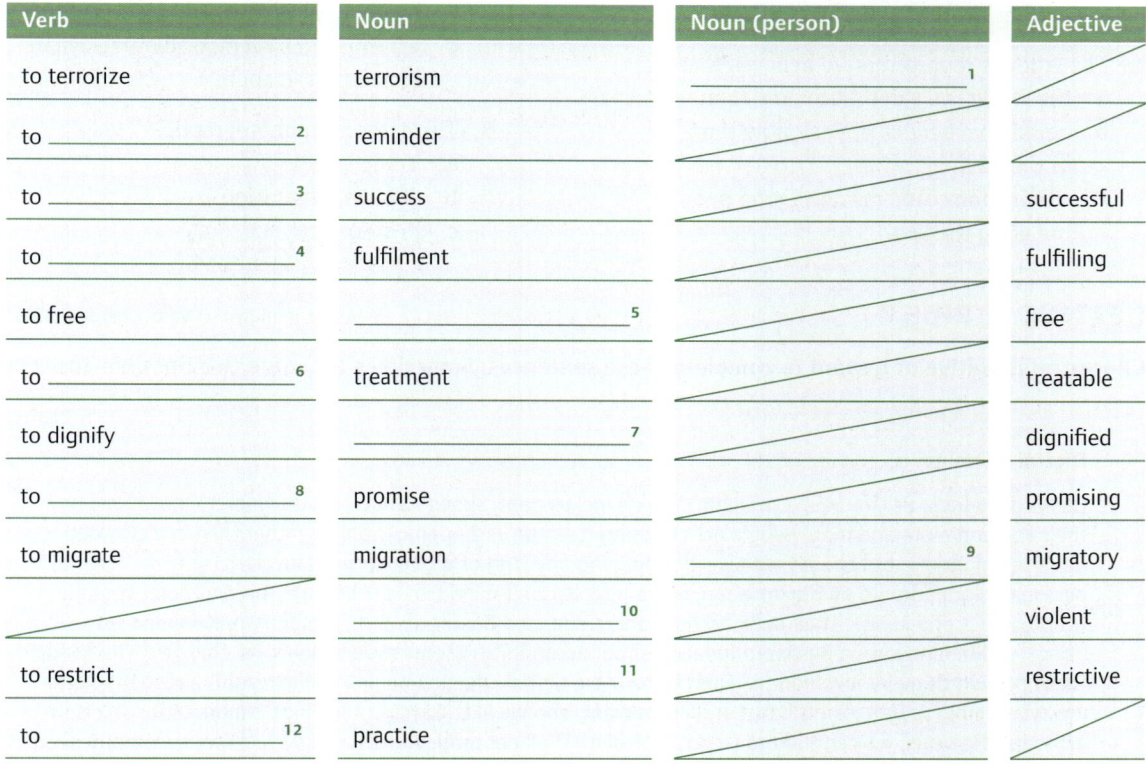

Verb	Noun	Noun (person)	Adjective
to terrorize	terrorism	_____ ¹	
to _____ ²	reminder		
to _____ ³	success		successful
to _____ ⁴	fulfilment		fulfilling
to free	_____ ⁵		free
to _____ ⁶	treatment		treatable
to dignify	_____ ⁷		dignified
to _____ ⁸	promise		promising
to migrate	migration	_____ ⁹	migratory
	_____ ¹⁰		violent
to restrict	_____ ¹¹		restrictive
to _____ ¹²	practice		

B Use ten of your answers in A to complete the text below. Make any necessary changes.

It is all too easy to see the young women who run away to _____¹ their dreams in Iraq or Syria as dangerous _____² just like the armed Islamic fundamentalists we often see on TV. It may seem strange but, just like other teenagers, they are simply rebelling and looking for their _____³. They find that the _____⁴ placed on Islam by Western society (e.g. the burqa ban) make it impossible for them to _____⁵ their religion in the way they wish. They expect to be treated with _____⁶, but the mass media's Islamophobia _____⁷ them every day that they do not belong. Some young Muslim girls actually _____⁸ in reaching the caliphate and arrive expecting that the people there will _____⁹ them with respect. Many are then shocked by the extreme _____¹⁰ of the ISIS fighters, but by then it is too late to leave.

4 LISTENING

→ Rezeption: Hörverstehen, SB S. 225

13

Listen to the radio talk show about surveillance cameras and complete the sentences with a, b or c.

1 The policeman feels that surveillance cameras are
  a the best way of identifying people who break the law.
  b one of several ways of identifying people who break the law.
  c an unacceptable way of identifying people who break the law.

2 The journalist
  a totally agrees with the policeman.
  b totally disagrees with policeman.
  c agrees with some of what the policeman says.

3 The actor is willing to give up
  a some of his safety for the sake of privacy.
  b some of his privacy for the sake of safety.
  c neither his safety nor his privacy.

4 The student representative believes that
  a the world is a safer place now than in the past.
  b people have more privacy now than in the past.
  c surveillance cameras don't stop people breaking the law.

5 The student representative
  a believes the police are quite capable of breaking the law.
  b had her phone hacked by the police.
  c was injured by a mounted policeman at a demonstration.

6 The actor hit a photographer
  a in the street.
  b at a demonstration.
  c in a hospital.

5 GETTING IT RIGHT

→ Verb + infinitive ▪ Verb + gerund, SB S. 262

Choose an infinitive or gerund to complete these sentences. Sometimes there are two possible answers.

Digital dilemma

Banks encourage us (to open / opening)[1] an online account, shops want us (to download / downloading)[2] their app and more and more people are choosing (to shop / shopping)[3] online rather than in a crowded department store – but there's a downside. Opening any kind of digital account involves (to give / giving)[4] personal information to an organisation. Some people don't mind (to do / doing)[5] this and don't hesitate (to provide / providing)[6] their bank account and credit card details. Experts therefore recommend (to use / using)[7] a different, strong password for each of our accounts and some even suggest (to change / changing)[8] these passwords every few months. This is where the digital dilemma begins. At first sight, a modern digital lifestyle seems (to be / being)[9] fast and convenient, and we like (to have / having)[10] more time for leisure activities. However, we can't afford (to lose / losing)[11] all our money to data thieves, so we constantly need to change our passwords. One way to avoid (to have / having)[12] all this stress is to buy things in shops again and use paper for our bank transactions.

6 BUILDING SKILLS

→ Interaktion, SB S. 246

Use the expressions in the box to fill in the gaps in the discussion. You can look at the *Useful language* on the back flap of the student's book if you need help.

> Do you see what I mean? ▪ I couldn't agree more! ▪ I see what you mean ▪
> I'm afraid I can't accept ▪ I'm sorry to interrupt, but ▪ If you ask me ▪ Let me put it in another way ▪
> So, is the basic idea that ▪ The main reason is ▪ There's some truth in what you say ▪
> Well, as a matter of fact ▪ What's your view on

Listeners are phoning in to speak on the BBC radio talk show *World have your say*. The topic for discussion is surveillance cameras.

Talk show host … Just stay on the line for a moment will you, Ronald? Let's hear what our next caller thinks. It's Margaret in Ireland. Why do you think we need more surveillance cameras, Margaret?

Margaret _____[1], people are more out of control these days, especially young people, so we need cameras in schools as well.

Talk show host And why are they out of control, Margaret?

Margaret _____[2] that school doesn't give them enough to do, so they do stupid things in their free time.

Talk show host _____[3] surveillance cameras in schools, Ronald? Is it a place where young people have too much free time and are out of control?

Ronald	_____⁴! Margaret's exactly right! We should have cameras in schools.
Talk show host	We should have surveillance cameras in schools, say Margaret and Ronald. Our next caller is Noureddine in Morocco. Do you agree with Margaret and Ronald?
Noureddine	_____⁵, I don't. Schools are a place of learning where people must feel free. They shouldn't be a place where 'Big Brother is watching you', so _____⁶ the idea that we need to keep control of young people with surveillance cameras.
Talk show host	So what do you say to Noureddine about that, Margaret?
Margaret	_____⁷ because young people need *some* freedom. A school shouldn't be like a prison, so _____⁸. But I do believe there isn't enough discipline. _____⁹: Imagine if you sent your child to your local school and found out they were doing drugs at lunchtime. You'd be really worried, wouldn't you? So _____¹⁰? You think your children are learning what they need for life and all they're doing is learning to break the law!
Talk show host	_____¹¹ if you give young people too much freedom, they'll break the law, Margaret? If you really believe that …
Noureddine	_____¹² I think that what Margaret is suggesting is completely wrong …

BUSINESS OPTIONS

A **Match one word from box A with one word from box B to make collocations. All the collocations are from page 134 of the student's book.**

A
overwhelming ▪ dysfunctional ▪ repetitive ▪ summer ▪ study ▪ healthy

B
hours ▪ work ▪ leave ▪ eating ▪ exhaustion ▪ attitude

B **Now use the collocations to complete the text below.**

I knew that I was heading for burnout when I had a feeling of _____¹ several times a week when I got home from work. I had been working at the same job for many years and the

_____² was becoming more than boring. I had noticed before that a lot of my

colleagues had a _____³ and it made the work environment quite unpleasant. I decided to speak to my boss about the problem and she came up with some very good ideas to help not only me but the whole department. She decided to have fruit baskets delivered to the office on a weekly

basis to encourage _____⁴ and she established _____⁵ so that people could leave work earlier when the weather was nice and sunny. A few people in the past asked

if they could have _____⁶ to learn new skills and although she unfortunately wasn't able to grant the time off, she did decide to bring some workshops to the office so that people could learn new skills during office hours. All these changes have been very positive and things are much better at work now.

1 WORKING WITH WORDS

Each of the first sentences contains a word from pages 136 and 137 of the student's book in *italics*. Complete the second sentences with a word with a similar meaning from the box. Make any necessary changes.

appear ▪ grow ▪ hugely ▪ lift ▪ opportunity ▪ reason for ▪ stop

1 Developing countries all aim to *raise* their levels of economic activity. By doing this, they can _____ their people out of poverty.

2 With China's rapid rise as a great economic power, its industries have developed *massively*. As we would expect, the country's energy needs have also increased _____ .

3 What's the *cause* of the increasing levels of CO_2 in the atmosphere? Most climate scientists agree that human activity is the main _____ this worrying change.

4 What happens if we can't *prevent* CO_2 levels from reaching 560ppm? If we don't _____ that from happening, most scientists say that disastrous climate changes will follow.

5 It's hard to be sure, but climate change *seems* to be happening already. For example, we _____ to get more wet weather in winter than we used to.

6 During the heaviest rains that have ever been recorded, the rivers *expanded* to twice their normal size last year. And the lakes _____ to three times their usual area.

7 The next international meeting on climate change offers another *chance* to control global CO_2 emissions. And that will give the world another _____ to limit climate change.

2 GETTING IT RIGHT

→ Indirect speech, SB S. 266

A **Report part of a debate on climate change. Use full forms of the reporting verbs in the simple past. (Some are in brackets, others are underlined.)**

Sally Miller:
(state) Climate change is nothing new because it's happening all the time: it always has done, and it always will. So I don't think that the Greens can blame humans for something that's just part of nature.

Mark Farina:
I don't agree. (point out) There's a clear connection between the rise in CO_2 levels that began with the Industrial Revolution and the warming that the world has seen since then. (go on to say) The more CO_2 people throw into the atmosphere, the more temperatures will continue to rise.

Sally Miller stated that climate change was nothing new because it was _____

_____

_____

_____

_____

_____

B Rewrite the questions as indirect questions, using the reporting verbs in brackets. (The reporting verbs should be in the simple past.) Make any other changes that are necessary.

Back in London after the Brussels trip, Julie's friends had lots of questions.

1 **Kate:** 'Does your newspaper often send you on jobs like that?' (ask)

Kate asked if her newspaper often _____

_____

2 **Chris:** 'How long were you away?' (want to know)

_____

3 **Lisa:** 'Did you interview anyone interesting?' (wonder)

_____

4 **Ellie:** 'What did you talk to Matt Radley about?' (inquire)

_____

5 **Tom:** 'Did he answer your questions properly?' (ask)

_____

6 **Jean:** 'Have you written your report yet?' (inquire)

_____

7 **Tom:** 'When can we read it in the paper?' (want to know)

_____

8 **Ben:** 'Where do you think they'll send you next?' (wonder)

_____

C Rewrite the requests, instructions and advice in indirect speech, using the reporting verbs in brackets. Make any other changes that are necessary.

The Brussels trip had been Julie's first big job, so her editor Tony Good wanted a meeting about it. He called Julie and said, 'Come to my office for a chat as soon as you're free.' (tell … to) 'Could you give me a bit longer so that I can finish my report?' Julie replied. (ask … to) So Tony gave her a time, and he also said, 'Email me the report before you come to let me have a quick look at it.' (requested … to) Julie agreed, and then she said, 'Perhaps you could suggest ways I can improve it.' (ask … to)

The Brussels trip had been Julie's first big job, so her editor Tony Good wanted a meeting about it. He

called Julie and told her to come to his _____

Julie asked _____

So Tony gave her a time, and he also _____

_____

_____

Before the meeting, Tony contacted the Features Editor, Tania Ray, and asked, 'Would you like to come to my office to discuss Julie Branson's report?' (invite … to) Both the editors liked the report, but Tony said to Julie, 'I think you should reduce it by about 100 words so that we can include a visual.' (advise … to)

Then he called Alan Carter in the Art Department and said, 'I want you to prepare a visual that will show the fracking process.' (instruct … to) Finally, at the end of the meeting, Julie made a big request. She said, 'Tony, could you send me to find out how local people feel about the fracking project? Please!' (beg … to)

Before the meeting, Tony contacted the Features Editor, Tania Ray, and _____

_____

Both the editors liked the report, but Tony _____

_____

_____

_____

_____

_____

3 **LISTENING**

→ Rezeption: Hörverstehen, SB S. 225

14

Julie interviewed local people 1–6 about the fracking project. Listen to their opinions. Then match the opinions a–f to the speakers.

a
It's essential to reject the fracking project because of constant noise from heavy vehicles and because of the danger of accidents.

Jenny Wade, student & Greenpeace supporter

Stella King, office worker & expecting 1st child

b
Although it will cause temporary local problems, it will bring investments that will produce permanent future benefits.

c
It will make a few rich people even richer, but will bring nothing but trouble to the whole community.

Lyn Benson, nursery teacher & mother of two

Brian Fox, 78, retired builder four-time grandfather

d
It's wrong to develop new fossil fuel sources. It's essential to rely just on renewable energy sources to protect the future of the Earth.

e
It's fine to accept some temporary problems as everything will be quiet and peaceful for many years after that.

Alan Smith, 20, apprentice mechanic

Bob Lowe, jobless engineering worker & father of three

f
Renewables cannot produce enough energy yet, so it's very important to generate power till then from a cleaner source than coal or oil.

4 **WRITING**

→ Produktion: Schreiben, SB S. 228

A The six opinions in 3 are different answers to issues a–c. Match two opposite opinions on each issue.

a Fracking's temporary effects: how important are they? (Opinions _3b_ & ___)

b Who gets what out of the project? (Opinions ___ & ___)

c Fossil fuels – or green renewables? (Opinions ___ & ___)

B Write three paragraphs for Julie Branson's report, one about each issue in 4A. Choose from these reporting verbs, and connect the opposite opinions with *However*, …

> accept ▪ argue ▪ believe ▪ complain ▪ feel ▪ think

Start like this, and continue in your exercise book.

What do local people think about the fracking project? I found that opinions were very varied, and here are just a few of them. Stella King, an office worker who is expecting her first child, thought that it was essential to reject the fracking project because of the constant noise from heavy vehicles and the danger of accidents. However, Bob Lowe, …

BUSINESS OPTIONS

Match the words in the box with their opposites (1–12). They are all from page 146 of the student's book.

> remove ▪ mend ▪ scale down ▪ benefit ▪ run out ▪ earn ▪ forward ▪ share ▪ add ▪ spend ▪ increase ▪ lend

1 add
_____

2 break
_____

3 have too much
_____

4 spend
_____

5 decrease
_____

6 take away
_____

7 keep for yourself
_____

8 save
_____

9 backward
_____

10 buy more
_____

11 borrow
_____

12 burden
_____

1 WORKING WITH WORDS

A Add vowels (a, e, i, o, u) to form two-word expressions from page 147 of the student's book.

1 grnhs gss _____

2 clmt chng _____

3 nvrnmntl plltn _____

4 glbl wrmng _____

5 ntrl rsrcs _____

6 crbn mssns _____

B Use expressions from A to complete the following text.

When the Industrial Revolution began using _____

_____ [1] such as coal and various metals for the mass

production of goods, it was quickly clear that it caused terrible

_____ [2], poisoning land, air

and water in the area. However, it now seems that human activities

are also causing much wider damage. Burning fossil fuels is producing

_____ [3] in the form of gases,

and these _____ [4] are raising worldwide temperatures. This is

_____ [5], and it appears to be leading to _____

_____ [6], which is likely to have disastrous effects on the world's weather systems.

C Complete the texts with words from the boxes – they are all from pages 147–149 of the student's book.

> ecosystems ▪ forests ▪ exploitation ▪ agriculture ▪ crops ▪ species ▪ farmland

From the earliest systems of _____ [1] nearly 10,000 years ago, this vital industry has

grown so much that it now requires the _____ [2] of over a third of the planet's land

area as _____ [3] in order to feed today's huge human population. Over the years, farmers

have cleared _____ [4] and many other natural environments with their ancient wildlife

_____ [5] to make room for food _____ [6] and animal _____ [7] that are

suitable for meat production.

> infrastructure ▪ cooperation ▪ groundwater ▪ diet ▪ consumption ▪ famine ▪ drought ▪ irrigation

Farming requires huge amounts of water, and this requirement keeps growing as the human _____ [8]

moves towards greater meat _____ [9]. Where there is no easy access to rivers or lakes,

farmers often pump _____ [10] to the surface and use that. Again, in dry areas where

_____ [11] is a problem, the _____ [12] of many people may be needed to build

a large _____ [13] of _____ [14] channels such as the system that carries

water from northern to southern California. If water supplies fail, the effects can be disastrous, as we have

seen in parts of Africa. Food can no longer be produced, so _____ [15] and death soon follow.

2 GETTING IT RIGHT

→ Participles, SB S. 268

Expand and connect the notes. Use the words in column 1 followed by participle clauses.

1	While	(grow up) / London	Joe Dean (love) going / help / aunt & uncle on / farm in / country / school holidays
2	Then before	(go) / college / age / 18	(spend) / summer as / volunteer on / organic farm
3	While	(study) economics for / next three years	(take) summer gardening jobs / make money
4	Before	(get) / 'proper' job at / end of college	(volunteer) / six months at CEFS (Centre for Eco-friendly Farming Studies)
5	Then after	(join) / big financial organization / London	(specialize) / investing in environmentally-friendly agriculture
6	After	(continue) with / work / several years	(start) dreaming / leaving & running / own project
7	Then while	(visit) / aunt & uncle, now in their 60s,	(begin) talking / his ideas & they (invite) him / run / farm for them
8	Since	(take over) / aunt & uncle's farm	(introduce) organic farming & / lot / new techniques

Start like this: *While growing up in London, Joe Dean loved going to help his aunt and uncle on their farm in the country in the school holidays. Then before ...*

3 WORKING WITH WORDS

A **Add these words from pages 147–157 of the student's book to the mind map.**

crops ▪ disease ▪ drought ▪ fertilizer ▪ GM technology ▪ herbicide ▪ hydroponics ▪ livestock ▪
organic practices ▪ pests ▪ pollution ▪ runoff ▪ selective breeding ▪ vertical farms ▪ weeds

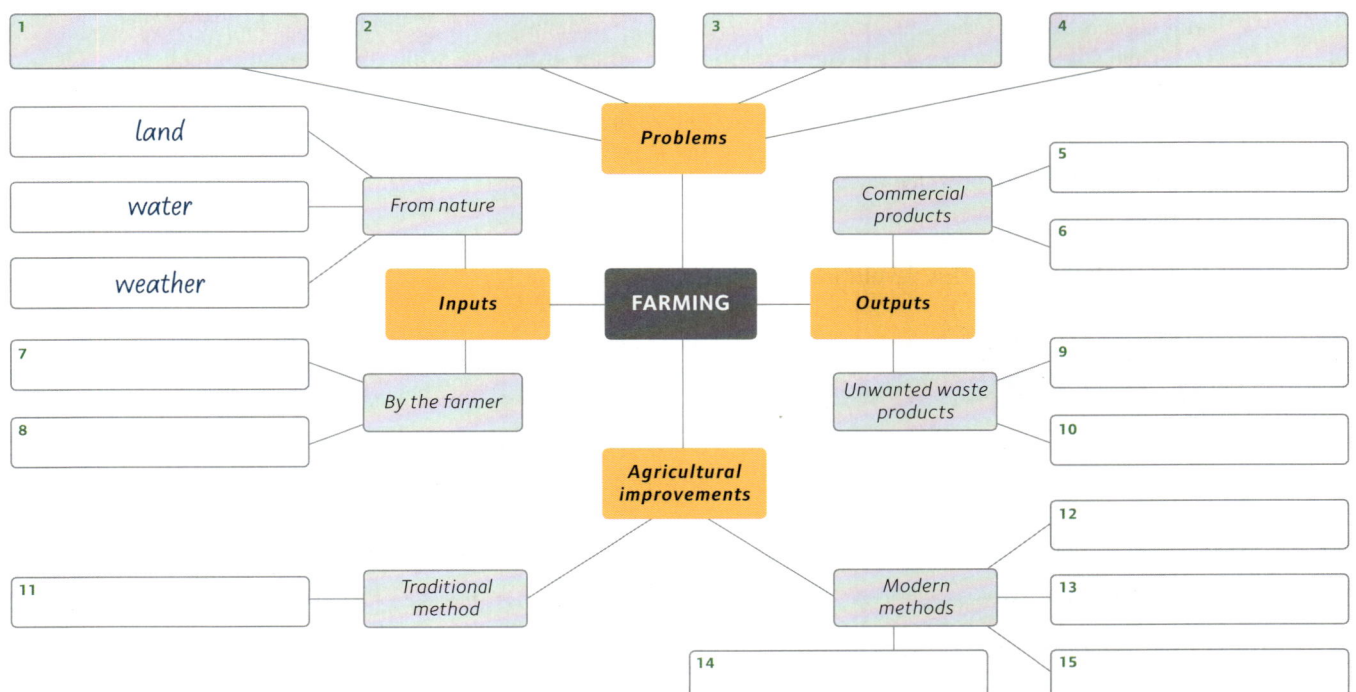

15 Feeding the world

B **Now complete these statements with words from the mind map.**

1 Inputs to farming from nature include land, water and _____[1], while inputs by the farmer include _____[2] and _____[3].

2 There is always a danger of damage and destruction, and the farmer faces many _____[4] such as _____[5], _____[6], _____[7] and _____[8].

3 The intended commercial products of farming consist of _____[9] and _____[10], but there are also _____[11] which include _____[12] and _____[13].

4 Farmers are always trying to make _____[14]. One traditional method has always been _____[15], while modern methods also include _____[16], _____[17], _____[18] and _____[19].

4 GETTING IT RIGHT

→ Participles, SB S. 268

Change the relative clauses (starting with *who*, *which*, *that*) to *~ing* or *~ed* clauses.

For over 200 years, there have been people who have said that famine would soon kill millions and who have predicted a great reduction in the human population. For example, enormous
5 famines that were predicted in the 1960s for India* and other parts of the world did not happen. Certainly, the scenes of African starvation which have often been shown on our TV screens have been real and terrible enough.
10 However, the fact is that scenarios which warned of hundreds of millions of deaths have not come true – at least, not yet.

This is largely thanks to a green revolution that was created just in time by new varieties of
15 rice, wheat and other crops. These are varieties that were developed by selective breeding in the 1960s and that produce far more food per acre with much greater reliability than before.

However, the productivity push that was
20 given to farming by this revolution is coming to an end, even while the population goes on rising rapidly. The race that is continuing ever more urgently today is to create a new green revolution to get us through the next half century. (190 words) 25

* See e.g. *The Population Bomb*, Paul Ehrlich, published 1968.

For over 200 years, there have been people saying that famine would soon kill millions and _____

_____

_____

_____

_____

_____

_____

58

5 LISTENING

→ Rezeption: Hörverstehen, SB S. 225

You and your friend are students in London and do not have much money for food. Listen to nutrition expert Dr Sally Carter on the radio as she explains two options.

A Listen to part 1 of the recording and complete the list of prices.

Fast-food prices

2 burgers	£ _____	
2 portions of French fries	£ _____	**Total**
2 colas	£ _____	**£ _____**

Supermarket prices

2 portions of chicken	£ _____	
½ kilo of potatoes	£ _____	
Vegetables	£ _____	
Fruit	£ _____	**Total**
1 litre of milk	£ _____	**£ _____**

B Listen to part 2 of the recording and complete the answers to the question: 'Why might people prefer to eat fast food?'

a Some people love _____

c Others don't know _____

b Other people don't like _____

d Fast food takes _____

C Listen to part 3 of the recording and complete the notes to answer the question: 'How much time might the two types of meal take?'

Type of meal	Activity		Time (minutes)	
A Fast food	a	Going there & back	15	
	b	_____	_____	Total
	c	_____	_____	_____
B Home-cooked	a	_____	_____	
	b	_____	_____	
	c	_____	_____	Total
	d	_____	_____	_____

Unscramble the anagrams below to find words from page 158 of the student's book. Then write down their German equivalents.

1 STVA _____

2 QTERNUEF _____

3 SPRION _____

4 VALICINI _____

5 TECILOEN _____

6 STLETE _____

7 GROUDTH _____

8 SIEVLKOCT _____

9 NONCTISTIOUT _____

10 CROFED BOULAR _____

11 SDILACEP _____

12 VERPOTY _____

1 WORKING WITH WORDS

Find words from pages 160 and 161 in the student's book, including the keyword (14).

1 The digital revolution has given us ▆ to information from all over the world.
2 Can I borrow your ▆ to call Ben? I've left mine at home.
3 If you become a ▆ , you'll learn how to write instructions that operate computers.
4 I can't talk now, so could you send me an ▆ with your suggestions?
5 'View' is an important ▆ . It lets you see text in different ways on your screen.
6 I don't use books much: I go ▆ to do most of my research.
7 I haven't got much cash with me, so I'll pay with my ▆ card.
8 If you want to change the print size, ▆ here at the top of the screen.
9 Send Lyn a text ▆ : it's cheaper than phoning.
10 I'm taking my ▆ with me so that I can keep working on the train.
11 At home, we get all our phone, TV and Internet services from just one ▆ .
12 Celtel built up a large ▆ of agents and engineers working across many parts of Africa.
13 The ▆ allows us to share information and communicate with anyone else anywhere.

Keyword: _____

2 WORKING WITH WORDS

A Complete the following. Use these words all starting with *re-*, meaning 'again'.

> rebuild ▪ redevelop ▪ remind ▪ reproduce ▪ rethink ▪ rewrite

1 It was embarrassing when I forgot her name again, and I had to ask her to _____ me.

2 Scientists all over the world are copying our experiments in order to try to _____ our results.

3 The fire damaged the clinic very badly, but they're going to _____ it just as it was before.

4 The digital revolution is changing Africa, and we must _____ our ideas about development.

5 These old 1960s office buildings are terrible. We should pull them all down and _____ the area as a shopping centre.

6 I produced the report before the new information came in. Now I need to _____ it completely.

B Form words that you know with these prefixes meaning 'the opposite of': *in-*, *im-*, *il-* and *ir-*.

_____ dependent   _____ legal   _____ possible

_____ formal   _____ literate   _____ regular

C Use opposites from B to complete the following.

1 **A** I suppose it'll be _____impossible_____¹ to contact you in Kenya.

   B Oh no, it's _____² to use the Internet there now.

2 **A** Do farmers have to be _____¹ to be able to use the iCow app?

   B No, it uses voice messages rather than text to help farmers who are _____².

3 **A** Intersat is still an _____¹ company, isn't it?

   B Yes, but it relies on other organizations in various ways. For example, it's _____²
   on TechStar for customer technical support.

4 **A** I hear that out in the villages there were only _____¹ visits by the community
   nurse two or three times a year.

   B Yes, but her visits are much more _____² now – nearly every month.

5 **A** It used to be _____¹ for farmers to sell the animals without any paperwork.

   B Right, but not anymore. That's _____² now, and every animal has to have ID.

6 **A** I hate _____¹ meetings where everyone wears suits. Do I really have to go?

   B Don't worry. They told me that this meeting would be relaxed and very _____².

3 **GETTING IT RIGHT**

Each sentence contains one mistake. Underline it and then correct it.

1 **A** Oh, no! It's 10.30, and Sue waits for my call – but my phone is dead!
   B Well, I'm lending you mine if you like.

2 **A** I hear Jamie must go to the Berlin IT-conference last week.
   B Yes, work was very, very busy, but luckily he could get there for a day.

3 **A** What did Carl do since I last saw him?
   B He's at college for the past six months.

4 **A** We only need to take few things with us.
   B Yes, I'm just packing two shirts, two trousers and one or two other things.

5 **A** Our contract was sign by the company and every member of staff.
   B Yes, and it clearly says that we must be pay for all our extra work.

6 **A** Is it true that the train went already when you got to the station?
   B Yes, so I did some work while I have been waiting for the next one.

7 **A** When I saw Liz last week, she told that she would visit us today.
   B Yes, but she now is planning to come tomorrow.

8 **A** Have you gone to Hawaii last summer?
   B No, but I spend two weeks there next summer.

4 LISTENING

→ Rezeption: Hörverstehen, SB S. 225

The radio show *The World This Week* is holding a debate about driverless cars, and the audience are being asked to give their views.

A Read the list of six jobs in the box below. Then listen and match four of them to speakers 1–4. Add their jobs to column 2.

18

> road construction company director ▪ Accident & Emergency (A&E) hospital nurse ▪ car repair workshop owner ▪ city planning officer ▪ in-car entertainment designer ▪ car insurance salesperson

Speakers	Names & job titles	Opinion	Views on driverless cars
	1 Sylvia Ray	☐	**a** Against: reduce demand for / company's services / cause unemployment in / industry
			b For: offer new opportunities / develop communication / other technologies / help drivers use / free time
	2 Ben Miller	☐	**c** For: cut / amount of space wasted on city parking / driverless cars / finish one job / go straight to another
	3 Julie North	☐	**d** For: greatly reduce / number / road accidents / save precious medical resources / deal / other needs
			e Against: not / possible / repair expensive hi-tech vehicles when / break down / destroy many small businesses like his
	4 Peter Hill	☐	**f** Against: if / really so safe / cut / cost / insurance / lots / people working / car insurance business / need to retrain

B Read the notes a–f in column 4. Then listen again to the views of speakers 1–4 and match the correct summary notes to the speakers in column 3 'Opinion'.

18

5 WRITING

→ Produktion: Eine Stellungnahme schreiben, SB S. 234

A Write a comment in two paragraphs. In paragraph 1 agree with one of the speakers from exercise 4. In paragraph 2 disagree with one of the other speakers. Use these ideas:

I (dis)agree with *(name)*, the *(job)*. I (do not) think … are (an excellent / a terrible) new technology, and I feel (he / she) is (right / wrong) to be (for / against) them. I really (do not) (believe / think it matters a lot) that *(view)* …

_____

_____

_____

_____

_____

_____

_____

_____

B Use the notes in column 4 of exercise 4 to write a paragraph that contrasts a 'for' and an 'against' idea. Structure it like this:

The *(job)* is for driverless cars, but the *(job)* is against them. On the one hand, the *(job)* is (worried / excited) that … On the other hand, the *(job)* is (excited / worried) that …

_____

_____

_____

_____

_____

_____

_____

_____

_____

BUSINESS OPTIONS

Unscramble the words to make questions and then answer them. All the answers can be found on page 170 of the student's book.

1 bathrooms / map / when / turn / do / the / green / on / the / ?

_____

2 created / who / live / the / map / ?

_____

3 design / app / encourage / what / is / to / the / of / the / supposed / do / ?

_____

4 Houghton / out / why / kicked / was / ladies' / of / room / the / ?

_____

5 sinister / app / what / about / is / the / ?

_____

6 Houghton / plans / software / does / sell / have / to / the / ?

_____

1 WORKING WITH WORDS

Complete the text with words from the box. The words are all on pages 175 and 176 of the student's book.

personalization ▪ ability ▪ creepy ▪ invasion ▪ related ▪ suit ▪ retailers ▪ uncomfortable ▪
consumer experience ▪ recommended ▪ purchase ▪ special offers ▪ bargain ▪ advert

My friend and I have different opinions about online shopping and the _____

_____[1] of shopping websites to _____[2] your

needs. My friend knows what she wants and goes to the websites she is familiar with to

_____[3] the things that she wants. She doesn't like to spend a lot of

time looking around and trying to find the best _____[4]. For this

reason, she likes _____[5] items that pop up on her screen while

she's shopping. She feels like the _____[6] understand her likes and

dislikes and their _____[7] to present her with

_____[8] that are perfect for her makes the process so much easier.

I have a very different opinion. When I am shopping online and I suddenly see an _____

_____[9] for something _____[10] to what I've been

searching for, I find it _____[11]. I feel like it is an

_____[12] of my privacy and I immediately want to leave the

website. I know that these online shops want to make my _____[13]

easier but it makes me so _____[14] that I don't shop online very

much anymore and prefer to just go to a store.

2 SENTENCE STRUCTURE

The words in these questions are mixed up. Put the questions in the correct order and then write a one sentence answer to each question.

1 see / shopping / Do / when / you / adverts / ?

_____

_____

2 adverts / Are / helpful / the / ?

_____

_____

3 find / you / creepy / Do / the / adverts / ?

_____

_____

4 sometimes / emails / offers / Do / get / you / special / with / ?

_____

_____

3 WORKING WITH WORDS

Complete the puzzle with the translation of the German words below. The words all come from the listening exercise on page 177 of the student's book.

1 unangemessen

2 scheinen

3 annehmen

4 buchen

5 gelegentlich

6 Gutschein

7 Geschäftsführer/in

8 Ausweis

9 Termin

10 tragen

11 regelmäßig

12 auftragen

Built-in obsolescence

1 WORKING WITH WORDS

A Match words 1–8 and a–h to make word pairs from the topic.

1	repair	**a**	down
2	even	**b**	attitudes
3	note	**c**	operation
4	in	**d**	shop
5	survey	**e**	upgrade
6	private	**f**	though
7	smartphone	**g**	details
8	consumer	**h**	sheet

B Now complete the sentences below with the word pairs from part A. Make any changes necessary.

1 Taking a broken device to an independent _____ could be cheaper but it is not always possible because of how the device is built.

2 Every time a device breaks and you decide to get a new one, it is very important to make sure that your _____ are deleted from the old one – just because it's broken for you, it doesn't mean someone can't get at your information.

3 The company asked their customers to fill out a _____ to learn more about what the people buying their product wanted so that they could improve the design.

4 Before buying a new device, it is important to _____ which features are the most important to you so that you don't spend a lot of money for features that you don't want or need.

5 If you choose to get a _____ every time a new device comes out on the market, you will be buying a new product every year. That costs a lot of money!

6 If a company builds products that do not stay _____ for more than three or four years, the company will lose customers who don't want to buy products that break so quickly.

7 _____ have a big influence on how products are built – if no one bought products that broke after a year or two, the manufacturer would have to change their model.

8 In order to have the newest gadget, many consumers choose to buy a new mobile phone _____ the one that they have still works.

2 WORKING WITH WORDS

Find synonyms of the words or phrases below in the topic on pages 178–180 in the student's book.

1 inexpensive   ☐☐E☐☐

2 easily broken   ☐R☐☐☐☐☐

3 chic   ☐☐☐☐☐I☐☐

4 thin   ☐L☐☐

5 former, preceding   ☐☐E☐☐☐☐☐

6 long-lasting   ☐☐☐☐☐L☐

7 expensive   ☐☐☐T☐☐

3 DESCRIBING A CARTOON

→ Cartoons beschreiben und analysieren, SB S. 236

Look at the cartoon and then comment on its meaning. Which problem is the cartoonist addressing and how does he/she do it? Write four or five sentences.

"We don't call it planned obsolescence anymore, we call it an upgrade."

4 ODD ONE OUT

Choose the word in the group that doesn't belong. Use a dictionary if necessary.

1 slim ▪ thin ▪ small ▪ big
2 earlier ▪ after ▪ previous ▪ before
3 change ▪ keep ▪ transform ▪ alter
4 fix ▪ break ▪ crack ▪ damage
5 durable ▪ strong ▪ weak ▪ dependable

3 Saturation from advertising

1 WORKING WITH WORDS

A Complete the table with the English equivalents of the German expressions. The expressions are all in the text *"It's just another funny animal video"* on pages 181 and 182 of the student's book.

1 _____	jdn aus dem Hinterhalt überfallen
2 _____	nach hinten losgehen
3 _____	jds Aufmerksamkeit auf sich ziehen
4 _____	Malerei
5 _____	Kriegsführung
6 _____	Reklamesendung
7 _____	Entkommen
8 _____	Erlaubnis
9 _____	projizieren
10 _____	unvergesslich
11 _____	preiswert
12 _____	Gerücht

B Now use the words and expressions from part A to complete the text below. Make any changes necessary.

I think comparing certain kinds of marketing to guerilla _____ [1] is a

perfect way to describe some of the advertising being presented these days. I often feel

_____ [2] on my way to and from work. Whether the advertising is done

with _____ [3] like graffiti or _____ [4] as a

picture or video, it's impossible not to notice it and you can't get away from it. I also think it's terrible that

companies often don't get _____ [5] before they decide to put their

advertising on the sides of buildings as this seems very disrespectful of private property. Some people, like

my sister, think this kind of advertising is really _____ [6] and interesting

and she argues that it's better for the environment than getting _____ [7].

She always thinks it's really cool the way companies create a _____ [8]

around their product and if things get really popular online, the company gets really

_____ [9] exposure. I, however, just find it frustrating. I feel like there is no

_____ [10] from it and to me, this kind of advertising

_____ [11] on the company because it makes me not want to buy their

product. I guess it certainly _____ [12] but not always in a good way.

2 WORKING WITH WORDS

Read the sentences below and then circle the word in brackets that best fits the context.

1 I am sometimes overwhelmed by the amount of advertising in my _____ .
(surround / surrounded / surroundings)

2 The company chose to only include white models in their advertising campaign and were therefore
accused of _____ marketing. (racism / race / racist)

3 Models have become so thin these days that I think it is very important to
_____ on whether or not advertising influences young people to strive for an
unrealistic physical ideal. (reflect / reflection / reflected)

4 When my car broke down, I didn't have enough money to buy a new one, so I felt quite
_____ to be offered a very inexpensive car with advertising painted on the
side. (luck / lucky / luckily)

5 The company made a mistake when it _____ to invest money in online
advertising. (neglected / neglect / neglecting)

6 The CATS _____ organized an advertising campaign to replace all the
billboards with pictures of cats. (collect / collective / collection)

7 One person who lived in the area was _____ ¹ by the cats but because she
likes dogs so much, she would have found puppies more _____ ². (amusing /
amused / amuse)

8 Some advertising campaigns are presented in order to _____ about important
issues rather than to try and sell something. (be aware / was aware / raise awareness)

3 WORKING WITH WORDS

**Use words from the listening exercise on page 183 of the student's book to write a brief description of
the pictures below.**

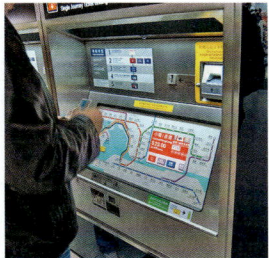

1 _____ 2 _____ 3 _____

4 _____ 5 _____

1 WORD FAMILIES

A Complete the table below. You can use a dictionary for help. The words are all from the article *Business leadership: One size can never fit all* on pages 184 and 185 of the student's book.

Noun	Verb	Adjective
collaboration	_____ 1	_____ 2
_____ 3	bore	_____ 4
_____ 5	_____ 6	prioritized
exclusion	_____ 7	_____ 8
_____ 9	bully	_____ 10
_____ 11	_____ 12	adopted
_____ 13	sound	_____ 14
filter	_____ 15	_____ 16

B Now complete the text below with words from the table. Make any changes necessary.

When my company decided to switch from a hierarchical organization to a flat organization, we were all excited. The plan _____ 1 great and we were really excited not to have to wait so long for information to be _____ 2 through the organization for decisions to be made. Many of us felt _____ 3 and unmotivated working on our own and our boss always told us what tasks we had to _____ 4 and get done first so we imagined that having a _____ 5 team where colleagues worked together would be more motivating. We thought we'd be more independent. Well, we were more independent, but with the independence, some employees started to _____ 6 their colleagues. I was really shocked but it really became a problem, especially in the form of _____ 7.

When we were forming teams for special projects, some of the colleagues were very mean because they didn't want to work with specific people. Thankfully this problem was quickly solved by the _____ 8 of some very clear guidelines.

2 WORKING WITH WORDS

A Match the words from bubble A with words from bubble B to create collocations from pages 184 and 185 of the student's book.

A

be

trouble   make

run   iron

self

power   like   fit

one size

try

in

B

out

smoothly   structure

minded   fits all

contrast

maker   vocal

motivated

happen

out

in

1 _____   7 _____

2 _____   8 _____

3 _____   9 _____

4 _____   10 _____

5 _____   11 _____

6 _____   12 _____

B Now match the collocations from part A with the German translations below.

1 Machtgefüge _____

2 reibungslos laufen _____

3 eigenmotiviert _____

4 Störenfried _____

5 sich lautstark äußern _____

6 ausprobieren _____

7 ausbügeln _____

8 hingegen _____

9 Einheitsgröße _____

10 gleichgesinnt _____

11 etwas in die Tat umsetzen _____

12 hineinpassen _____

1 SENTENCE STRUCTURE

Rewrite these sentences using the words in the box to replace the underlined sentence parts. Make any necessary changes. The words are all from the text *When companies tie (and untie) the knot* on pages 187 and 188 of the student's book.

> headquarters ▪ assess ▪ pay off ▪ handbook ▪ more effort ▪
> incompatible ▪ insecure ▪ profitable

1   By merging the two companies, the owners thought that they would <u>earn more money</u>.

_____

2   Although there were branches in London and New York, the <u>main office was</u> in Paris.

_____

3   The boss had to rearrange the offices because two of the colleagues sharing an office <u>did not get along</u>.

_____

4   Once a year, I have a meeting with my boss in which she <u>tells me what I do well and what I can improve upon</u>.

_____

5   All of the new employees at our company receive a <u>folder</u> when they start which gives them information about who works for the company and what the standard procedures are.

_____

6   I felt <u>very nervous</u> when I first started the job, but the longer I worked there, the more I understood my tasks and after a few weeks, I felt much better.

_____

7   Putting in <u>extra hours</u> to make sure the project was finished on time <u>was</u> definitely <u>worth it</u>.

_____

2 WORKING WITH WORDS

Read the sentences below and then circle the word in brackets that best fits the context.

1   The two companies came together hoping that they could share ideas, (experts / expertise / exercise) and headquarters.

2   When a high-end company merges with a company that offers a more (economical / economics / economy) vehicle, problems can arise.

3   If a bigger company (imposed / imposing / imposes) all of their ideas on the smaller one, some of the employees could become angry.

4   If an idea is bad, it's often better to just (scrap / scrappy / scrapped) it rather than to continue to try even though it's obvious it's not working.

5   Everyone will be happy if the merger (pays off / pays up / pays on).

6   Many of the employees, who liked to wear jeans to work, were angry when the new bosses suddenly said there would be a formal (dress order / dress code / dress formula).

7 Often small details that seem (insignificantly / significant / insignificant) end up being extremely important.

8 Human Resources is responsible for (stabilization / stabilizing / stable) the mood in the company and making sure differences are addressed in a productive way.

9 If the marriage (or merger) turns out to be (unhappy / happy / unhappiness), it can end in divorce.

10 If you don't address (unsolved / solved / unsolvable) problems, they will become even bigger problems in the future.

→ Rezeption: Leseverstehen, SB S. 214

3 **LOOKING AT THE TEXT**

A **Read the texts in exercise 6 on page 189 of the student's book and then complete the sentences below.**

1 Many colleagues in the Spanish company were nervous about …

_____

_____

2 The Spanish colleagues thought that their new German colleagues were …

_____

3 The Spanish employees were concerned that …

_____

4 The German colleagues were frustrated with their new Spanish colleagues because …

_____

5 The German colleagues found their Spanish colleagues' behaviour disrespectful because …

_____

6 When the German colleagues tried to talk about problems, the Spanish colleagues …

_____

B **Which work environment, the Spanish or the German, would you like to work in? Write three sentences explaining your point of view.**

_____

_____

_____

1 WORKING WITH WORDS

A Match the words in column A with words in column B to make collocations. All of the words can be found on pages 190–192 of the student's book.

COLUMN A	COLUMN B	
1 locally	A sourced	_____
2 junk	B market	_____
3 human	C conscience	_____
4 job	D governance	_____
5 fair	E food	_____
6 regulatory	F customer	_____
7 professional	G world	_____
8 clear	H ethics	_____
9 corporate	I rights	_____
10 social	J floor	_____
11 developing	K responsibility	_____
12 end	L body	_____
13 labour	M practices	_____
14 factory	N trade	_____
15 business	O development	_____

B Now use ten of the collocations from part A to complete the text.

_____ [1] is something that many people have decided is important in their shopping and working life. Because of this, _____ [2] has become necessary. People want to buy their products with a _____ [3] and are therefore careful to make sure that the _____ [4] of people working in the _____ [5], who work for low wages on the _____ [6], are not violated. Many products are now labelled with _____ [7] logos so that the _____ [8] knows that the product was produced with ethical _____ [9]. Some people, however, believe that _____ [10] products are the most important and therefore choose to purchase items from their own area rather than products shipped from abroad.

2 WORKING WITH WORDS

Find words in the text *Is corporate social responsibility good business?* on pages 190–191 of the student's book that match the definitions below.

1 the people who own stock in a company _____

2 satisfaction _____

3 whole _____

4 healthy _____

5 to keep a supply of sth to sell _____

6 food that is not good for you _____

7 to tell someone not to do something _____

8 official acceptance _____

3 MUDDLED SENTENCES

The sentences A–M got mixed up. Number them 1–13 in the correct order to create a blog entry. The first sentence is given for you.

☐ **A** When I go to a big supermarket chain, I always check to see where my fruits and vegetables come from and I try very hard to only buy local food.

☐ **B** There are often two different kinds in my supermarket, one kind from South Africa and one from Italy.

☐ **C** But either way, it is a positive change for the environment.

☐ **D** Since Italy is much closer to my home than South Africa, I choose to buy the Italian grapes.

☐ **E** For example, I live in northern Europe and I don't buy bananas very often because there is no place in continental Europe where they can be grown.

☐ **F** Instead, they are being pushed by the consumer.

☐ **G** Grapes are another good example.

☐ **H** That means that if I do buy bananas, they have been flown half way around the world to get to my supermarket and that is not good for the environment.

☐ **I** In the end, I guess the store is not really being socially responsible on their own.

☐ **J** If the most important thing for the supermarket is to make money and people stop buying products from far away, the supermarket will either lose money on those items or choose to stock other items in their store that people will buy.

☐ **K** Most big corporations are only out to make money.

☐ **L** For me, it is very important to be aware of how my purchases affect the environment.

☐ **M** That means that the way that I and other people spend their money has a big influence on how companies work and what products they sell.

7 Population, wealth and refugees

1 WORKING WITH WORDS

Complete the crossword with words from pages 194 and 195 of the student's book.

1		organization that gives money or help to people in need
2		when too many people live in an area
3	(across)	a situation when people have no or little food over a long period of time
3	(down)	run away
4		not likely to happen
5		economic system based on private ownership
6		two times
7		boring
8		a place to live or somewhere where people are protected from weather/danger
9		person with new ideas
10		unfair treatment of someone based on race or religion
11		person fleeing their home country

2 LOOKING AT THE TEXT

→ Rezeption: Leseverstehen, SB S. 214

A Read the text *A prominent economist destroyed the argument against re-homing refugees across Europe* on pages 194 and 195 of the student's book and say if the following statements are true (T), false (F) or not in the text (N). Correct the false statements.

	T	F	N
1 Legrain thinks that refugees put a huge strain on the economy of their new country.	☐	☐	☐
2 Legrain believes that the influx of refugees can be good for the EU.	☐	☐	☐
3 The additional spending on refugees in the EU could cause a recession.	☐	☐	☐
4 Countries with low immigration have low economic growth.	☐	☐	☐
5 Refugees often do the work that local people find boring.	☐	☐	☐

B Now use the same text to complete the following sentences.

1 Many people are worried about the large number of refugees coming into the EU because … _____

_____ .

2 Legrain believes that refugees can help the economy by … _____

_____ .

3 If people are able to move to more technologically advanced and politically stable countries, … _____

_____ .

4 The fastest areas of employment growth in advanced economies are … _____

_____ .

5 Countries with high birth rates or high immigration have higher economic growth because … _____

_____ .

6 Legrain wishes that policy makers would … _____

_____ .

3 WRITING A COMMENT

→ Produktion: Eine Stellungnahme schreiben, SB S. 234

Write a short paragraph explaining why you agree or disagree with Philippe Legrain's point of view about refugees. Use words and phrases from the box to help you write your text.

> concerned ▪ taxpayers ▪ well-developed ▪ asylum seekers ▪ hopelessness ▪ influx of ▪
> skill level ▪ economic growth ▪ desperation

_____

_____

_____

_____

_____

_____

_____

8 The future job market

1 WORD FAMILIES

A Complete the table below with vocabulary from the topic in the student's book. You can use a dictionary for help.

VERB	ADJECTIVE	NOUN
memorize		_____ 1
_____ 2		advertisement
_____ 3	demanding	_____ 4
_____ 5	advanced	_____ 6
prolong	_____ 7	_____ 8
customize	_____ 9	_____ 10
_____ 11	personalized	_____ 12
communicate	_____ 13	_____ 14
orbit	_____ 15	_____ 16
_____ 17	_____ 18	amazement
	_____ 19	pain

B Now complete the text below using words from part A. Make any changes necessary.

When looking for a job and going through the job interview process, there are a few things you need to remember. When you see a job _____ [1] and decide that you would like to send in your CV, you must make sure that you _____ [2] it and your cover letter. If the person reading these introductions feels that you have not sent a _____ [3] letter, they will probably throw it away and you will not get an interview. Once you have been invited for an interview, make sure that you really prepare yourself. Otherwise the process can be quite _____ [4]. Take time to _____ [5] a few facts about the company and practise your interview techniques, making sure that you are able to _____ [6] why you are a good fit for the position. The process can be difficult and you shouldn't be _____ [7] if you have to do several interviews before you feel truly comfortable. However, once you've done a few, you'll find that you are more comfortable and companies will be _____ [8] that you come and work for them.

2 WORKING WITH WORDS

A Match words from group A with words with group B to create collocations. All the words can be found on pages 196-198 of the student's book.

GROUP A		GROUP B	
1	entry	a	language
2	open	b	guide
3	tour	c	opening
4	body	d	science
5	storage	e	up
6	set	f	guidelines
7	medical	g	labour
8	silent	h	work
9	physical	i	part
10	body	j	level
11	job	k	observer
12	manual	l	capacity

B Now match the collocations with their German translations.

1   eröffnen _____

2   offene Stelle _____

3   Einstiegs- _____

4   körperliche Arbeit _____

5   Medizin _____

6   Körpersprache _____

7   Reiseführer/in _____

8   Richtlinien aufstellen _____

9   Körperteil _____

10   Lagerkapazität _____

11   Handarbeit _____

12   stiller Beobachter _____

3 ODD ONE OUT

Read the words and phrases and then decide which one does not belong to the rest of the group. Give a reason for your decision.

1   interviewer ▪ applicant ▪ observer ▪ job opening

_____

2   physical work ▪ receptionist ▪ engineer ▪ tour guide

_____

3   customized ▪ body parts ▪ organs ▪ legs

_____

4   neuroscientist ▪ medical scientist ▪ bio-engineer ▪ pianist

_____

1 WORKING WITH WORDS

A Look at the article *How Silicon Valley Shapes Our Future* on pages 199–200 of the student's book and then find 7 verbs, 5 adjectives and 6 nouns from the text in the word puzzle.

N	O	I	T	I	T	E	P	M	O	C	D	W	N	Q	V	V	I
Q	B	R	E	A	T	H	T	A	K	I	N	G	I	M	D	M	C
Y	W	Z	O	Z	Q	F	U	D	E	T	E	R	M	I	N	E	C
E	S	U	O	I	R	U	F	F	R	V	R	S	K	F	A	I	F
T	R	L	D	E	Z	H	Q	J	A	Q	T	A	F	K	O	D	N
J	R	X	Z	T	T	S	X	J	R	J	K	Y	Q	N	E	E	Z
M	J	A	Y	L	I	A	T	V	C	U	W	W	T	F	N	W	L
A	E	W	N	U	A	K	L	N	L	R	T	L	U	O	O	A	A
N	R	I	J	S	Q	I	V	O	E	G	E	H	R	T	W	P	T
K	U	T	V	N	P	R	D	W	I	T	V	D	L	L	O	F	E
I	T	N	A	I	L	O	A	K	M	V	E	K	C	E	R	E	I
N	P	E	P	L	R	L	R	C	C	H	U	P	M	A	S	K	C
D	A	S	M	N	T	T	K	T	K	O	B	I	M	X	T	S	O
R	C	S	B	E	R	D	O	N	A	N	M	E	X	O	N	E	S
O	R	K	R	T	Y	T	G	V	C	T	W	Q	T	V	C	J	I
S	S	E	N	I	Z	A	R	C	F	O	I	R	H	L	J	N	N
C	D	G	H	B	Q	J	Z	U	R	L	X	O	K	V	N	F	I
V	P	P	E	P	C	R	H	K	Q	R	J	Y	N	I	P	R	N

VERBS	ADJECTIVES	NOUNS
1 _____	1 _____	1 *competition*
2 _____	2 _____	2 _____
3 _____	3 _____	3 _____
4 _____	4 _____	4 _____
5 _____	5 _____	5 _____
6 _____		6 _____
7 _____		

B Now match the words from A to their German definitions below.

1	miterleben	_____
2	Drohne	_____
3	wütend	_____
4	bestimmen	_____
5	Verrücktheit	_____
6	verspotten	_____
7	Konkurrenz	_____
8	beleidigen	_____
9	atemberaubend	_____
10	schonungslos	_____
11	Rahmen	_____
12	Transport	_____
13	gesellschaftlich	_____
14	erobern	_____
15	verändern	_____
16	unfähig	_____
17	Menschheit	_____
18	verletzen	_____

C Now complete the sentences with words from A. Make any changes necessary.

1 The development of electric cars will greatly _____ our dependence on oil.

2 People who were born in the first half of the 20th century cannot believe the technological developments that they are _____ today.

3 There are new _____ being developed that can fly into disaster and war areas carrying food so that no human lives are put at risk.

4 The future of our planet will be _____ by how quickly we are able to change our dependence on fossil fuels and start using more sustainable fuels.

5 Our governments need to create a strong _____ of standards to make sure that technology does not violate our privacy.

6 Technological advances have caused a lot of _____ change and the way we live and communicate has changed drastically from how our parents lived.

7 The _____ between internet companies is _____ . Every company wants to be the first with a new product, whatever the cost.

8 Leading companies are trying to _____ markets all over the world.

1 WORKING WITH WORDS

A Complete the texts below with the English equivalent of the words in brackets. The words are all from the text *A marriage of giants* on pages 202 and 203 of the student's book.

1 There is a big _____ (Streit)[1] right now about genetically modified food. To be honest, I don't really see what the big deal is. Most of us, at some time in our lives, have eaten foods that have had some sort of genetic modification. No one has found any _____ (langfristige)[2] health problems related to it and I don't understand where this _____ (weit verbreitete)[3] negativity comes from. People should stop _____ (unterbinden)[4] the use of genetic modification. It can help many people by, for example, creating plants that are less _____ (verletzbar)[5] to certain insects so that _____ (Bauer)[6] don't have to use so many _____ (Pflanzenschutzmittel)[7].

2 I am very careful about not buying genetically modified foods. I believe clear _____ (Kennzeichnung)[8] is very important so that people in the supermarkets can easily see what food they are buying. The potential problems are not truly _____ (bekannt)[9] and more research has to be done before _____ (Behörde)[10] can say what impact this food could have on human beings and the environment. By genetically altering seeds, we could be creating _____ (Komplikationen)[11] in nature that no one expected. The public _____ (Aufschrei)[12] should be listened to. Perhaps we will learn in the future that we were being too careful, but better that than _____ (auszulösen)[13] a problem that could have been prevented.

B Now say which text opposes genetic modification and which text supports it.

Text 1: _____   Text 2: _____

2 COMMENTING ON A CARTOON

→ Cartoons beschreiben und analysieren, SB S. 236

A Make notes on the following questions about the cartoon on the next page

1 What product is being referred to in the cartoon?

_____

2 What is the 'genetic engineering' the cartoon is talking about?

_____

3 What is funny or ironic about the cartoon?

_____

B **Now use your notes to describe the cartoon and comment on its message.**

_____

_____

_____

_____

_____

_____

_____

_____

_____

The miracle of genetic engineering

3 WORKING WITH WORDS

Some of the words in these sentences got a bit mixed up. Solve the anagrams to complete the sentences based on the text on pages 202 and 203 of the student's book.

1 The fear of a merger between two corporate giants in the pharmaceutical and chemical industries caused NIOMTLSTEVNRNEASI to get out and protest.

_____

2 Bernie Sanders, who ran for the democratic SENLTADPIREI MONAOTININ, tried to COBKL the merger between the two corporations.

_____   _____

3 The PIOTOPONIS to the merger was partly because of concern that the two companies would have a YPNOOLOM on ESED and smaller companies would be pushed FOF HTE RKMETA.

_____   _____

_____   _____

4 Some EU countries have already NABNED genetically modified seeds but others believe that these seeds are LEENEMRTAY to solving the problem of not enough food for a growing world population.

_____   _____

Sustainable agriculture

1 WORKING WITH WORDS

A Read the definitions a–q and then match them to the expressions 1–17. All the words are from *Coming together to feed the world* on pages 205 and 206 of the student's book.

1	surface		a	the top of a house
2	diminish		b	to help or make stronger
3	bee		c	saved money to be used for a special purpose
4	social housing		d	not poisonous
5	rise		e	having enough money
6	rooftop		f	the land along the edge of a sea or lake
7	fund		g	the land behind a house
8	supply		h	a person with psychological problems
9	well off		i	where chickens live
10	coop		j	having understanding or knowledge of a situation
11	mental health patient		k	less expensive housing supported by the state
12	sustain		l	to come to the top
13	awareness		m	to go up
14	shore		n	to get smaller
15	edible		o	an insect that makes honey
16	dweller		p	to provide sth
17	backyard		q	resident, inhabitant

B Now use the words and expressions from part A to complete the sentences below. Make any changes necessary.

My friend Helena works with underprivileged children who live in _____[1] and teaches them about gardening and sustainable agriculture. She helps the kids gain _____[2] of where their food comes from so that they will hopefully become responsible consumers. She doesn't only teach the kids, she also lives what she teaches. She has a chicken _____[3] of her own in her _____[4] and has a steady _____[5] of organic eggs. She also keeps _____[6] and she often invites her students to her home to show them what the hives are like and how to take care of them. She's now working on a project to put some hives on the _____[7] of the apartment units where the kids live in the city. She's in the process of raising _____[8] for the project and it looks like they'll be able to start it in a few months. Helena often talks about what a rewarding experience it is to work with these kids and watch their knowledge _____[9] to the point that they start telling their friends to be more careful with the world around them. The kids aren't _____[10] and they can't afford to go to expensive food stores, but as they learn more about sustainability, their apathy _____[11] and they begin to care more about what food goes into their bodies.

2 **LOOKING AT THE TEXT**

→ Rezeption: Leseverstehen, SB S. 214

Read the text *How can I help the planet by not eating meat?* and write suitable headings for the six sections. The first one has been done for you.

HOW CAN I HELP THE PLANET BY NOT EATING MEAT?

1   *Not eating meat can help the planet*

The process of raising animals for food uses up a large amount of natural resources (e.g. food, energy, land and water) and is considered by many to be a big problem in the fight against climate change. Some people focus on the treatment of animals that are being raised for meat, while others care more about the environmental impact. Either way, eating less meat is one of the simplest things you can do to help improve the world's environment.

2   _____

The environmental impact of raising animals for meat has a big influence on rainforest destruction. Two acres of rainforest are cleared every second and much of this land is used for cows. In Latin America, 75 per cent of land that used to be rainforest is now used for cattle ranching and in the United States, much of the land that used to be forest is now used to grow food for these animals.

3   _____

Not everyone wants to be a vegetarian but even if you just choose to eat vegetarian meals for one day a week, it can help. There are studies that say if every American skipped just one meal of chicken once a week, it would have the same environmental impact as taking 500,000 cars off the road.

4   _____

The way that animals like chickens, pigs and cows are raised for food creates a very large amount of greenhouse gases that are leading to climate change. It's not just the raising of the animals but also the transportation of the animals and the meat which contribute to the bad influence on the environment. And meat consumption is growing so the impact will be even worse in the future.

5   _____

In the United States, the amount of waste that the animals create is more than the human population of the world. There are no places to filter the animal waste so, on many farms, the waste just sits in pools and creates pollution. If the excrement is not processed, it can pollute water and air and cause health problems for the people living close to the farm.

6   _____

About 50 per cent of the food we grow is given to animals that are being raised for meat. This food could be given to people who live in places where there is not enough food. Studies show that it takes about 10 kilos of grain to create just one kilo of meat. The land that is now being used to grow grain for the animals could instead be used to grow vegetables for people who do not have enough food.

12 Industrial Revolution 4.0

1 WORKING WITH WORDS

A Find words from the text *Industrial Revolution 4.0* on pages 208 and 209 of the student's book in the puzzle that match the German words below.

D	C	K	I	Z	G	H	L	M	J	I	W	P	K	T	U	N
S	H	X	L	P	P	O	N	J	C	C	G	I	T	H	S	V
L	M	G	K	M	I	M	P	L	E	M	E	N	T	O	M	P
X	K	W	I	U	H	S	I	L	B	A	T	S	E	J	P	R
E	P	R	R	T	E	K	C	O	P	N	R	E	T	T	A	P
Y	X	A	L	N	N	Z	T	K	E	F	J	K	W	B	V	G
L	E	N	E	R	G	E	T	I	C	Q	H	C	Z	I	S	L
S	T	O	P	T	I	M	I	Z	A	T	I	O	N	O	Y	N
S	P	W	T	G	I	S	J	I	Y	S	T	L	N	M	H	F
E	S	A	K	S	L	L	A	C	I	D	A	R	H	E	L	S
L	X	W	P	X	E	V	O	L	V	E	B	J	E	T	V	R
M	T	B	I	E	O	R	N	W	R	E	K	C	A	R	T	E
A	V	E	Y	P	R	E	R	R	S	E	G	X	D	I	P	J
E	S	D	Z	A	E	L	N	G	N	K	H	E	M	C	P	H
S	D	R	W	Q	P	A	E	J	M	S	K	T	U	F	U	O
M	A	T	T	R	E	S	S	S	O	O	P	E	E	L	S	E
A	L	Z	N	W	R	H	Y	W	S	Y	Q	C	V	S	E	T

1 biometrisch _____

2 aktiv _____

3 genießen _____

4 einführen _____

5 überhaupt _____

6 sich entwickeln _____

7 realisieren _____

8 Schloss _____

9 Matratze _____

10 Optimierung _____

11 papierlos _____

12 Muster _____

13 Tasche _____

14	drastisch	_____
15	Erholung	_____
16	reibungslos	_____
17	bestimmt	_____
18	Schlaf	_____
19	wischen	_____
20	Überwachungsgerät	_____

B **Now use words from part A to complete the following text. Make any necessary changes.**

It is difficult to keep up with the _____[1] changes that are happening in our

technological society today. As soon as you buy a new smart phone, the technology has

_____[2] and it's already time to buy a new one. It can feel like money is falling

out of your _____[3]! Sometimes it feels like these advances are positive: the

_____[4] of _____[5] billing, for example, has been very

simple and significantly reduces the amount of paper waste. Devices that are used as

_____[6] to help people to remember to exercise have also had a positive impact

on personal health. The downside, however, is that we sometimes have trouble getting enough

_____[7] and _____[8] because we spend so much time in

front of the computer that our brains find it difficult to switch off after a long day. And even though there

are many forms of _____[9] that make life easier, the question is: are we

_____[10] a culture where privacy doesn't exist anymore?

2 BRAINSTORMING

Look at the four Industrial Revolutions listed below. Write one to three sentences describing how these revolutions affected people in their everyday lives.

1st Industrial Revolution – Steam Engine _____

_____

_____

2nd Industrial Revolution – Mass Production and Electricity _____

_____

_____

3rd Industrial Revolution – Digitalization _____

_____

_____

4th Industrial Revolution – Internet of Things and Artificial Intelligence _____

_____

_____

Track list

Track	Title/Exercise	Page
1	Title & credits	
2	Unit 1, Exercise 7B	6
3	Unit 2, Exercise 6	9
4	Unit 3, Exercise 4	11
5	Unit 5, Exercise 5	18
6	Unit 6, Exercise 3B	21
7	Unit 7, Exercise 6	27
8	Unit 8, Exercise 1	28
9	Unit 9, Exercise 5	34
10	Unit 10, Exercise 4	38
11	Unit 11, Exercise 4	42
12	Unit 12, Exercise 3	45
13	Unit 13, Exercise 4	49
14	Unit 14, Exercise 3	54
15	Unit 15, Exercise 5A	59
16	Unit 15, Exercise 5B	59
17	Unit 15, Exercise 5C	59
18	Unit 16, Exercise 4	62